AMAZING
QUESTIONS
KIDS ASK ABOUT
The Bible

DAVID R. VEERMAN, M.DIV.

JAMES C. GALVIN, ED.D.

JAMES C. WILHOIT, PH.D.

DARYL J. LUCAS

RICHARD OSBORNE

Tyndale House
Publishers, Inc.
Carol Stream,
Illinois

TYNDALE is a registered trademark of Tyndale House Publishers, Inc.

Tyndale's quill logo is a trademark of Tyndale House Publishers, Inc.

Amazing Questions Kids Ask about the Bible

Copyright © 1994 by The Livingstone Corporation and Lightwave Publishing, Inc. All rights reserved.

Illustrations by Lil Crump. "Jason and Max" © 1989 Impartation Idea, Inc.

Produced for Tyndale by Lightwave Publishing and The Livingstone Corporation

Scripture quotations are taken from *The Simplified Living Bible,* copyright © 1990 by KNT Charitable Trust. All rights reserved. Used by permission.

ISBN-13: 978-1-4143-0801-2
ISBN-10: 1-4143-0801-9

Printed in the United States of America

10 09 08 07 06
 6   5   4   3   2   1

CONTENTS

INTRODUCTION

THE BIBLE
 What is a Bible? **1**
 Did the Bible stories really happen, or are they like fairy tales? **2**
 When was the Bible made? **3**
 How many people wrote the Bible? **4**
 *What does **inspired** mean?* **5**
 Why are there four books about Jesus in the Bible? **6**
 Where did they get the scrolls from? **7**
 If lots of different people in different places wrote the Bible, how did it get together in one big book? **8**
 Why can't we put new books in the Bible? **9**
 Will people write about us in a special Bible, too? **10**
 Why do so many people keep translating the Bible? **11**
 Why isn't there just one kind of Bible? **12**
 *What is a **Living Bible**?* **13**
 Why did God put scary stories in the Bible? **14**
 Is archaeology the study of Noah's ark? **15**
 Why do we study the Bible? **16**
 How can kids study the Bible? **17**
 What's a concordance? **18**
 Why do we memorize verses? **19**
 Why is the Bible in two parts instead of in one part? **20**
 What is the Bible's biggest story? **21**

OLD TESTAMENT EVENTS AND PEOPLE
 How did God make people? **22**
 If Adam and Eve hadn't sinned, would people sin today? **23**

What made the Garden of Eden prettier than other gardens today? **24**

Why did Eve disobey God when she knew she would die? **25**

Why did Cain kill his brother? **26**

How did Noah build a boat that was so big? **27**

Why did God flood the whole earth? **28**

Why did God put a rainbow in the sky? **29**

Why did God choose Abraham to go to the Promised Land instead of someone else? **30**

Why was Abraham willing to kill his own son? **31**

Why did Jacob trick his dad? **32**

Why did Joseph's brothers sell him? **33**

Why didn't Joseph go back home? **34**

Why didn't the bush burn up? **35**

Why wasn't Moses afraid to go to Pharaoh? **36**

Why wouldn't Pharaoh let the people go? **37**

Why did God send plagues on Egypt? **38**

Why did the Israelites smear blood on their doors? **39**

How did Moses part the Red Sea? **40**

Why did God give Moses so many laws for the Israelites to obey? **41**

Why did the Israelites who left Egypt have to wander in the wilderness until they died? **42**

Did the Israelites have lawyers and courts for their judges? **43**

Was Samson a good guy or a bad guy? **44**

Why did Samson tell Delilah his secret? **45**

Why did Hannah leave her son at the church? **46**

Why did the people want to have a king? **47**

What did Goliath eat that made him so big? **48**

How did David fight Goliath if he was so small? **49**

Why was Saul jealous of David? **50**

Why did Solomon want to cut the baby in half? **51**

Were prophets the people in Bible days who made lots of money? **52**

Why did Elijah go up to heaven so early? **53**

Why did God send the Jews to Babylon? **54**

Whose hand made the writing on the wall? **55**

How did Daniel sleep with the lions without being afraid? **56**

Why didn't the Jews ever change their clothes while they were rebuilding the walls? **57**

What's a Maccabee? **58**

NEW TESTAMENT EVENTS AND PEOPLE

Why was Jesus born in a stinky stable? **59**

Did people in the Bible have Christmas? **60**

Why do angels light up and get bright? **61**

How come Zacharias couldn't talk until his son was born? **62**

Why did John the Baptist live in the desert? **63**

Why did the Holy Spirit come down on Jesus like a dove? **64**

How did Jesus do miracles? **65**

Are Beatitudes short for bad attitudes? **66**

If Jesus doesn't want us get hurt, why did he tell us to chop our hands off and poke our eyes out? **67**

What's a parable? **68**

Why did the disciples tell the people Jesus was too busy to see the kids? **69**

What does Passover mean? **70**

Why did Judas betray Jesus? **71**

Why were the Roman soldiers so mean? **72**

Why did the people say, "Come down off the cross if you are the Son of God"? **73**

Did Jesus know that he would come to life again? **74**

Why did Jesus go up to heaven instead of staying here on earth? **75**

Didn't the tongues of fire on the apostles' heads burn them? **76**

How could the angel unlock Peter out of jail without keys? **77**

How big were the worms that ate King Herod? **78**

How could Peter kill and eat animals that were in a vision? **79**

Why was it against the law to make friends with a Gentile? **80**

Why was Saul blinded by a bright light? **81**

Why did Paul want to tell the Romans about Jesus? **82**

How did Paul send letters to churches if they didn't have mailboxes? **83**

Why hasn't God told us when Jesus is coming back? **84**

Is there church in heaven? **85**

Will I have a bedroom up in heaven? **86**

BIBLE TIMES

When did all this happen? **87**

How did the people travel? **88**

Did children in Bible times color? **89**

Do people live in the land of Israel today? **90**

Why did people in Bible times bow down to welcome each other? **91**

Why did people go to wells instead of using the water at home? **92**

Did people have shoes in Bible days? **93**

How come there are no Bible stories that take place in winter? **94**

Did people have ice cream in Bible times? **95**

*How come the husbands could have so many
    wives?* **96**
Why did people kill animals for church? **97**
Did people in Bible times have music? **98**
Were there any crimes in the Bible? **99**
What language did they speak in Bible days? **100**
Does God have things to do at nighttime? **101**
Does God have a sense of humor? **102**

INTRODUCTION

The purpose of this book is to help you answer your children's questions about God's Word, the Bible.

Childhood is an ideal time to develop a thirst for God's Word, for children then will have a lifetime of discovering God's truths and applying them. But the Bible is often intimidating to children. Children can find the stories in the Bible virtually impossible to understand, considering that they think concretely, not conceptually like adults. In addition, young children think in real time; that is, they can't quickly put stories into the proper historical context. So they may wonder if the disciples had to fight dinosaurs or why they didn't just drive to Galilee.

Children love to ask questions. Most parents could spend hours telling about the continual stream of questions that flow from their children's mouths, especially the persistent, "Why?"

When a child asks a question, he or she needs to be heard and taken seriously. This is especially true in the spiritual area. It would be a grave mistake for a parent to leave a child's question unanswered or to treat it as a cute distraction, regardless of how simple or humorous it might seem. Beyond being cute, the questions are sincere attempts to find answers, to learn truth. And parents who take those questions seriously and help their children find answers move them closer to God and his Word.

This book is filled with real questions; that is, they were asked by real boys and girls. Out of scores of questions, we chose 102 to answer. The answers have been carefully thought through and crafted, not as the last, exhaustive word on the subject, but as thorough answers that young, inquiring minds can understand. Along with each answer, you will usually find related questions, key verses, and other Bible references.

This book will help you answer your children's questions about the Bible. But as you do so:

- Look for the question behind the question. For example, if a little girl asks, "Is there church in heaven?" (question 85), she may really be envisioning an eternity of singing hymns and listening to long sermons.
- Do not make up an answer when you don't have one or when the Bible is silent. For example, one parent answered this question (question 61), "Why do angels light up and get bright?" by saying, "Each angel has a star for a home." Doing that only pairs fiction with truth. Too often, children will lump the stories in the Bible with superstitions and fictions they've heard and later discovered to be false. Be honest with your answers. If you don't have an answer, say so. Or suggest that you look for the answer together.
- Be ready for follow-up questions. Your answer may lead to more questions. That's the mark of a good answer—it makes the child think.
- Make your answers concrete. Children think in very literal terms, so abstract concepts such as "heaven," "sovereignty," and "God's will" are difficult for them to understand until their ability to think abstractly naturally develops. Try to give simple answers to their questions, but focus on helping the children learn to pray,

read and memorize the Bible, and do what God wants.

- Always take children's questions about the Bible seriously, even when they sound funny to you. It's amazing what little eyes see and little ears hear.
- Show your child that the best place to look for answers to questions about the Bible is the Bible! If *you* go there for the answers, so will your kids.

Jesus said, "Let the little children come to me. Don't stop them. For the Kingdom of Heaven belongs to such as these" (Matthew 19:14). When your child asks questions, take the time to look up the answers together. Use this book as a tool to help you know where to find those answers.

As we carefully and lovingly answer our children's questions about the Bible, we can help them gain understanding and a love for God and his Word.

THE
BIBLE

Q: WHAT IS A BIBLE?

A: The Bible is God's message to us. Actually, the Bible is not just one book, but a collection of many books that have been put together. It came to be called *the* Book because it is so important, because it is *God's* book. (The word *Bible* means *book*.) The Bible serves as an instruction manual for living God's way; it tells us what's right and what's wrong. It has many stories and lessons that he wants us to know. The Bible tells us about God and Jesus and how we are supposed to live. You can look in the Bible to find out what God wants you to do.

KEY VERSE: *Your words are a lamp to light the path ahead of me. They keep me from stumbling and falling. (Psalm 119:105)*

RELATED VERSES: *2 Timothy 3:16-17; 2 Peter 1:16-21*

RELATED QUESTIONS: *What does the word **Bible** mean? Why are there sixty-six books? Why would God want to invent a Bible?*

Q: DID THE BIBLE STORIES REALLY HAPPEN, OR ARE THEY LIKE FAIRY TALES?

A: The stories in the Bible really happened. Some of the events seem amazing to us because they're miracles, but they still happened. We know that the stories are true because the Bible is God's Word, and God wouldn't lie to us or fool us. The Bible also says that every word in it is true. Some people don't believe the Bible because they haven't read it. Some don't believe it because they don't think miracles can happen. Others don't believe because they don't want to; they don't want to learn about God and do what he tells them to do. But we know that God can do anything, and he's the best one to tell us how to live. We should pray for those who don't believe the Bible or who think it's full of fairy tales.

KEY VERSE: *All these things happened to them as examples to us. They warn us not to do the same things. They were written so we could learn from them as the world nears its end. (1 Corinthians 10:11)*

RELATED VERSES: *Luke 1:1-4; John 20:29; 21:24-25; 1 John 1:1-4*

RELATED QUESTIONS: *How do we know that what the Bible says is true? How do we know the Bible stories are true? Why do some people think the Bible isn't real? Why don't some people believe the Bible? Are the stories about Jesus true?*

NOTE TO PARENTS: *This question presents a good opportunity to take out a Bible and look at it together.*

Q: WHEN WAS THE BIBLE MADE?

A: God wrote the Bible over many, many years, a long time ago—long before computers, cars, and even before books. The people who wrote down God's words used scrolls of paper made from papyrus leaves and animal skin. They wrote it over a period of 1,500 years, from the time of Moses to the apostle John. Even though the Bible was written hundreds of years before we were born, it is still up-to-date. When we read the stories and understand what God is saying, we learn how we should live today.

KEY VERSES: *Long ago God spoke in many different ways to our fathers. He spoke through the prophets in visions, dreams, and even face to face. Little by little he told them about his plans. But now in these days he has spoken to us through his Son. He has given his Son everything. Through his Son he made the world and everything there is. (Hebrews 1:1-2)*

RELATED VERSES: *2 Peter 1:16-21*

RELATED QUESTIONS: *Why didn't Jesus write the Bible for us? Why did God get Moses to write part of the Bible? Why did Moses only write five Bible books?*

Q: HOW MANY PEOPLE WROTE THE BIBLE?

A: God used many people to write the Bible. Moses, King David, and the apostle Paul wrote a lot. God also used prophets to write down his words—Isaiah, Jeremiah, and Ezekiel, to name a few. We also know that God used many different kinds of people—old, young, kings, apostles—with many different backgrounds and personalities. God used a lot of people to write the Bible because the events described in it took place over many, many years.

KEY VERSES: *No prophecy in the Bible was thought up by the prophet himself. The Holy Spirit within these godly men gave them true messages from God. (2 Peter 1:20-21)*

RELATED VERSES: *Jeremiah 36:2; Hebrews 1:1; 2 Peter 3:16*

RELATED QUESTION: *Why did God get so many people to write the Bible?*

Q: WHAT DOES INSPIRED MEAN?

A: *Inspired* describes the way God used the Bible writers to write down what he wanted them to write. (It doesn't mean "perspired.") It doesn't mean dictated; that is, God didn't say the words out loud while the writers copied them down. Inspired means that God guided the writers, helping them to write everything he wanted them to write, so that all the words in the Bible would tell us what we need to know. He gave the writers the ideas and the desire to write; then he guided them so that every word they wrote was what he wanted.

KEY VERSE: *The whole Bible was given to us by inspiration from God. It is useful to teach us what is true. It helps us to know what is wrong in our lives. It straightens us out and helps us do what is right. (2 Timothy 3:16)*

RELATED VERSES: *2 Peter 1:16-21*

RELATED QUESTIONS: *Who wrote the Bible—God or his followers? Why do we say the Bible is God's Word? How do we know that God wrote the Bible?*

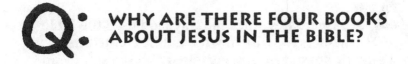

Q: WHY ARE THERE FOUR BOOKS ABOUT JESUS IN THE BIBLE?

Just One Gospel

BENEFITS
• Bibles will be more compact
• easier to read

PASTOR

A: The Gospels are the books in the Bible that tell us about Jesus' birth, life, death, and resurrection. God used *four* books because each book tells the story of Jesus from a unique point of view. Each one shows us something different about Jesus. When we read all the Gospels, we see the whole picture. It's like seeing a house from all four sides.

The four stories about Jesus are all named after their writers: Matthew, Mark, Luke, and John. Matthew and John knew Jesus, went places with him, and were his close friends; they were two of Jesus' original twelve disciples. Matthew was a tax collector; Mark was a friend of the twelve disciples; Luke was a doctor; John was a fisherman.

KEY VERSE: *Jesus did many other things as well that aren't recorded here. And if all of them were written down, the whole world wouldn't hold all the books! (John 21:25)*

RELATED VERSES: *Luke 1:1-4; John 20:30-31; 21:24-25*

RELATED QUESTION: *Who wrote Matthew, Mark, Luke, and John?*

NOTE TO PARENTS: *If this question arises, open your Bible and show your kids where the four Gospels are.*

Q: WHERE DID THEY GET THE SCROLLS FROM?

A: Today, we use pencils and pens to write, and we write on paper. But the Bible was written a long time ago, long before these things were invented. Instead of using paper, people would write on long strips of *papyrus* or *parchment*. Papyrus was made from a plant that grows in Bible lands. Parchment was made from animal skins. Both papyrus and parchment could be sewn together and rolled up into long scrolls. Museums have some of these ancient scrolls. People read from these scrolls like books. But there weren't a lot of them because each one had to be copied by hand. Today, everyone can have his or her own Bible to read. But in those days, most synagogues and churches would only have one copy each. So the scrolls were very valuable, and the priests took good care of them. We should take care of our Bibles, too.

KEY VERSE: *When you come, bring the coat I left at Troas with Carpus. Also bring the books, but especially bring the parchments. (2 Timothy 4:13)*

RELATED VERSE: *Jeremiah 36:2*

RELATED QUESTION: *Where did they get the Bible?*

Q: IF LOTS OF DIFFERENT PEOPLE IN DIFFERENT PLACES WROTE THE BIBLE, HOW DID IT GET TOGETHER IN ONE BIG BOOK?

A: The first books of the Bible, the Old Testament, were written to the Jewish people. The Jews took care of and protected these books and spent countless hours carefully copying them again and again. Jesus often quoted from the Old Testament and said it was all true and that it was the Word of God. The books that we find in the New Testament were written by people who had seen Jesus or who were close to those who had contact with Jesus. Their stories about Jesus (the Gospels) and their letters (the Epistles) were read in the local churches. Church leaders collected the writings and guarded them carefully. For nearly 2,000 years now, all these Bible books have been together.

KEY VERSE: *Yes, being a Jew is good. First of all, God trusted them with his laws. That way they could know and do his will. (Romans 3:2)*

RELATED VERSES: *Matthew 5:17-20; Mark 14:49; Luke 24:27-46; John 2:22; 5:39; 7:38-42; 10:35; 17:12*

RELATED QUESTION: *What happened to the letters that Paul wrote to the churches?*

Q: WHY CAN'T WE PUT NEW BOOKS IN THE BIBLE?

A: We can't put new books in the Bible because the Bible is *God's* message, not ours. It contains his words, which he inspired his people to write in a special way. Some people have tried to put new books in the Bible, but others who recognized that the Bible is a special book kept them from changing it. The story about how God has saved us is complete. God has already told us all we need to know and do.

KEY VERSE: *I have serious words for everyone who reads this book: Don't add anything to what is written here. If you do, God will give you the plagues described in this book. (Revelation 22:18)*

RELATED VERSES: *Hebrews 1:1-2*

RELATED QUESTIONS: *What if God tells someone to put new books in the Bible? What was wrong with the books that didn't make it into the Bible?*

NOTE TO PARENTS: *While Protestants and Catholics differ on the question of including the intertestamental books in the Bible, no Christian denomination is arguing for new books to be added to the Bible. Many heretical teachers and leaders have tried to add their words to those of Scripture. Many others have tried to give additional writings the same status as the books of the Bible. But God's people recognize that the Bible contains God's words, not our own, so it's not up to us what goes in it.*

Q: WILL PEOPLE WRITE ABOUT US IN A SPECIAL BIBLE, TOO?

A: There is only one Bible (or "revelation from God"), and it has already been written. But remember, the Bible is far more than a collection of stories about people who lived a long time ago—it's God's message about Jesus; it tells how we should live today. The Bible also tells us about the future, not just the past. So in one sense, we *are* in the Bible. We are important in God's plan. Also, the Bible tells us that those who believe in Jesus have their names written in the "Lamb's Book of Life"—that's another book that God has. It tells who will live with God in heaven.

KEY VERSE: *Nothing evil will be allowed into it. No one immoral or dishonest can be there. Only those who are written in the Lamb's Book of Life can enter the city. (Revelation 21:27)*

RELATED VERSES: *Psalm 119:129-133, 137-140*

RELATED QUESTION: *Why wasn't there a Bible written from the end of our Bible to now?*

Q: WHY DO SO MANY PEOPLE KEEP TRANSLATING THE BIBLE?

A: The Old Testament first was written in the Hebrew language, and the New Testament was written in Greek. If no one had ever translated the Bible, only people who could read ancient Hebrew and Greek would be able to understand the Bible today. Fortunately, over the years men and women have taken the time to put the Bible into other languages, including English, so that speakers of almost *all* languages can read it.

But some people still don't have the Bible in their own language—some don't even have a written language. For them to read God's Word, somebody has to put their language into written words. Then someone has to translate the Bible into their language so they can read it. Imagine if there were no Bibles in your language— how would you read it? God wants us to take the message about Jesus to everyone all over the world, and that means translating the Bible into every language there is. That's why people keep translating the Bible.

KEY VERSES: *"So now go and make disciples in all the nations. Baptize them into the name of the Father, the Son, and the Holy Spirit. Then teach these new disciples to obey all the commands I have given you. And be sure of this thing! I am with you always, even to the end of the world." (Matthew 28:19-20)*

RELATED VERSES: *Isaiah 6:8; 1 Timothy 4:13*

A: There are many kinds of Bibles because there are many kinds of people. But they all contain the same message. Different Bibles meet different needs. Some Bibles are very small so you can carry them with you. Others are big so you can see the words better. Some Bibles use everyday words to make the Bible easy to read and the lessons easy to learn. Some Bibles have notes, maps, and charts to help people understand the parts that are different from today. The purpose of all these different Bibles is to help people understand what God is saying so they can obey him.

KEY VERSE: *Until I get there, read and explain the Bible to the church. Preach God's Word. (1 Timothy 4:13)*

RELATED VERSES: *2 Timothy 2:15-16*

RELATED QUESTIONS: *Why doesn't the King James Version have the English that we speak in it? Why are some Bibles study Bibles and some aren't?*

NOTE TO PARENTS: *It is very important for children to have a translation of the Bible that they can read and understand themselves. If they ask this question because they can't understand their own Bible, consider getting them a translation that they can understand.*

Q: WHAT IS A **LIVING BIBLE?**

A: *The Living Bible* is an English version of the
Bible. The words and sentences in *The Living
Bible* reflect the way people speak today so that most
people can understand them. The Bible talks about the
Scriptures as being "living and active," so that's where
the name came from. There are many other English
translations of the Bible. Some of the most well-known
are: the New International Version, the *New American
Standard Bible,* the King James Version, the New King
James Version, and the New Revised Standard Version.

KEY VERSE: *For whatever God says to us is full of living
power. It is sharper than the sharpest sword. It cuts swift
and deep into our innermost thoughts and desires. It
shows us for what we really are. (Hebrews 4:12)*

RELATED QUESTIONS: *Why do they call **The Living Bible**
the Living Bible? Is the New King James written by a new
guy named King James? Is NIV the last name of the man
who wrote the Bible?*

Q: WHY DID GOD PUT SCARY STORIES IN THE BIBLE?

14

A: The Bible tells true stories about real people who actually lived and died. Sometimes those stories can seem scary to us. God included those stories because he wanted to teach us something from them. That is, they weren't put there to scare us but to serve as a warning of what to avoid, to show us what we should do, and to help us learn how to live. Some teachings in the Bible seem scary to people, especially people who disobey God, because the stories reveal the bad that can happen when we choose to do evil. Hopefully, these teachings will show us how important it is to listen to God.

KEY VERSE: *All these things happened to them as examples to us. They warn us not to do the same things. They were written so we could learn from them as the world nears its end. (1 Corinthians 10:11)*

RELATED VERSES: *Psalm 119:105; John 20:30-31; Revelation 1:3*

RELATED QUESTION: *Why did God tell us about all sorts of terrible things that happen?*

Q: IS ARCHAEOLOGY THE STUDY OF NOAH'S ARK?

15

A: Archaeology is the study of ancient cultures. It tells us about Bible times and people who lived long ago and what life was like back then. Archaeologists are the people who study and teach about archaeology. They find out about Bible times by digging up old cities to find buildings and things people used long ago. They are even trying to find Noah's ark. Archaeologists study other places, too, and have shown us many interesting things about people and places all over the world.

KEY VERSES: *So the flood slowly went away. And 150 days after it began, the boat came to rest upon the mountains of Ararat. (Genesis 8:3-4)*

RELATED VERSES: *Genesis 6:9–8:22*

RELATED QUESTIONS: *What is archaeology? How do we know about Bible times? Have they found Noah's ark yet?*

Q: WHY DO WE STUDY THE BIBLE?

16

A: It's important to study the Bible because the Bible is God's message to us and studying it helps us know and understand it better. If you want to learn more about butterflies, you study butterflies. Studying the Bible helps us find out how to live and to find out what God wants. When we only read the Bible (without studying it), we may not see the meaning right away. *Studying* helps us learn lessons for life—we learn God's will so we can obey him. Studying the Bible is like reading a story many, many times—each time you see something different and learn more.

KEY VERSE: *Work hard so God can say to you, "Well done." Be a good workman. Then you won't be ashamed when God examines your work. Know what his Word says and means. (2 Timothy 2:15)*

RELATED VERSES: *2 Timothy 3:16-17*

RELATED QUESTIONS: *How come God makes us do homework? What's doctrine? What's theology? Why do people have different ways of understanding the Bible?*

17

A: Studying the Bible is not as difficult as it may sound. In fact, it can be fun! First, start out by just reading the Bible. Read short portions—a paragraph or story—and read it in a translation you understand. Second, ask a parent to explain big words to you that you don't understand. Third, memorize verses that tell you what you should do. As you read and study, you will have questions about what the Bible means. Save your questions and find someone to answer them, like a parent, teacher, or pastor. It's good to read the Bible every day. Make it a habit. And if you get really ambitious, you can use a Bible dictionary and atlas; a dictionary tells what Bible words mean, and an atlas shows where Bible places are.

KEY VERSE: *"Always remind the people about these laws. You yourself must think about them every day and every night. That way you will be sure to obey all of them. For only then will you succeed." (Joshua 1:8)*

RELATED VERSES: *Deuteronomy 6:6-9; Joshua 1:6-8; Psalm 119:1-176; Proverbs 1:1-9*

RELATED QUESTIONS: *Should we study the Bible every day? Why does God want us to do homework? What's a running reference?*

NOTE TO PARENTS: *A child asking this question may provide a good opportunity to introduce him or her to study. Get out a Bible and start a study together. Some Bible books that many kids will find interesting include Genesis, Mark, Romans, and James. If you are unfamiliar with the Bible, you can use this book to help you get an overview.*

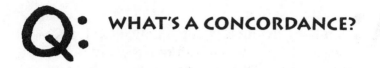

Q: WHAT'S A CONCORDANCE?

18

A:

A concordance is an index of words in the Bible. It lists the words that appear in the Bible and all the verses where those words appear. Many study Bibles include a concordance in the back. If you know part of a verse but don't know where to find it in the Bible, you can look up one of the verse's words in the concordance, and it'll tell you where the word is used. For example, if you want to find the verse, "God loved the world so much that he gave his only Son. Anyone who believes in him will not die but have eternal life," you could look up the word *believes* in the concordance. It would tell you all the places where *believes* is used, and you could see if any of them is the one you're looking for. For practice, see if you can find it now!

KEY VERSE: *Work hard so God can say to you, "Well done." Be a good workman. Then you won't be ashamed when God examines your work. Know what his Word says and means. (2 Timothy 2:15)*

RELATED QUESTION: *Why does Daddy use big books to study the Bible?*

Q: WHY DO WE MEMORIZE VERSES?

19

A: We memorize Bible verses because we want to remember what God has told us. When we have the Bible in our head, God's Word will be with us when we're out playing, at the pool, or doing anything—it's with us wherever we go. Then, when we face a problem or a tough situation, we will be able to remember what God has told us to do. It's also fun to memorize verses—then during the day, we can think about the verses and what they mean.

KEY VERSE: *Your words are a lamp to light the path ahead of me. They keep me from stumbling and falling. (Psalm 119:105)*

RELATED VERSES: *Psalm 119:11; 2 Timothy 2:15*

RELATED QUESTIONS: *Can we memorize the whole Bible? How can we memorize the whole Bible? What does meditating on the Bible mean?*

NOTE TO PARENTS: *Don't make Bible memorization feel like a chore, and never use it as a punishment for bad behavior. Instead, make it into a game. The goal is for children to **enjoy** reading the Bible and memorizing verses, not merely that they have a lot of Bible knowledge. Some good ones to start with include John 3:16, Genesis 1:1, and Romans 12:9.*

Q: WHY IS THE BIBLE IN TWO PARTS INSTEAD OF IN ONE PART?

20

A: The Bible has two main parts: the Old Testament and the New Testament. The Old Testament tells the story of the beginning of the world and the beginning of the nation of Israel. It also tells about how the people of Israel obeyed and disobeyed God over many, many years. All of the stories and messages from God in the Old Testament lead up to Jesus Christ. The New Testament tells the story of Christ, the early Christians, and the future. You can think of the Old Testament and New Testament as "before Christ" and "after Christ," or as volume 1 and volume 2. Old doesn't mean out-of-date—it means that it happened before Jesus. But remember, even though the Bible has two main parts, it is all one book—God's book.

KEY VERSE: *"You search the Scriptures, for you believe they give you eternal life. And the Scriptures point to me!" (John 5:39)*

RELATED VERSES: *John 10:35; 2 Timothy 3:14-15; Hebrews 1:1-2*

RELATED QUESTIONS: *Why is one called **old** and one called **new**? What is the Old Testament?*

NOTE TO PARENTS: *If your kids aren't already familiar with the two parts, pick up a Bible and show them the Old Testament and New Testament.*

Q: WHAT IS THE BIBLE'S BIGGEST STORY?

21

A: The Bible's biggest story is the story of Jesus. In fact, the whole Bible tells his story—about God creating people and saving them from sin. Jesus came to the world to die in our place, to pay the penalty for our sins. If we trust in Christ as Savior, God gives us eternal life. The Old Testament Bible writers told us that Jesus would be born, live, die, and rise again. Even the sacrifices described in the book of Leviticus show us what the death of Christ would be, the perfect "Lamb of God who takes away the sin of the world." No matter where you look in the Bible, you can learn about Jesus. Have you put your faith in him?

KEY VERSE: *"God loved the world so much that he gave his only Son. Anyone who believes in him will not die but have eternal life." (John 3:16)*

RELATED VERSES: *John 5:39; 20:31; Acts 4:12*

NOTE TO PARENTS: *The Bible's biggest story is also a parent's biggest responsibility. In order to be ready for the day when a child asks a question like this one, plan what you will say and which Scriptures you will use to introduce him or her to Jesus.*

OLD TESTAMENT EVENTS AND PEOPLE

Q: HOW DID GOD MAKE PEOPLE?

SCULPTURE
(not the way God did it)

22

A: The Bible tells us that God made Adam from the "dust of the ground." In other words, God took something he had already made, dust, and formed a man's body out of it and then gave that body life. God made Adam, the first man, just the way he wanted him. Then God made Eve from part of Adam, just the way he wanted her. We're all made by God. And he has made us just right.

KEY VERSE: *The time came when the Lord God formed a man's body. He made it from the dust of the ground. Then he breathed into it the breath of life. And man became a living person. (Genesis 2:7)*

RELATED VERSES: *Genesis 1:26-27; 2:21-22*

RELATED QUESTIONS: *How come God made Eve out of Adam's rib? What did God use to make people? Why did God only make people on earth and not on other planets? Why didn't God make the woman out of dust?*

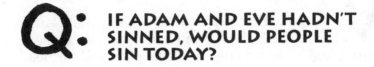

Q: IF ADAM AND EVE HADN'T SINNED, WOULD PEOPLE SIN TODAY?

23

A: We really don't know what would have happened if Adam and Eve hadn't sinned in the Garden of Eden, but their temptation was a very important test. Unfortunately, they failed the test, and sin entered the world; the perfect world became damaged, broken, and dirty. Because of Adam and Eve's sin, every person who has ever lived has been born a sinner. Sin is passed on from parents to their children. We do wrong things because we're sinners.

KEY VERSE: *Adam caused many to be sinners because he disobeyed God. Christ caused many to be welcome to God because he obeyed. (Romans 5:19)*

RELATED VERSES: *Romans 5:12-19*

RELATED QUESTION: *Would Satan still be here on earth trying to get people to be evil if Adam and Eve hadn't sinned?*

NOTE TO PARENTS: *Though Adam and Eve sinned, God made a way for all people to come back to him—to be forgiven—by sending Jesus.*

Q: WHAT MADE THE GARDEN OF EDEN PRETTIER THAN OTHER GARDENS TODAY?

24

A: The Garden of Eden was more beautiful than any garden today because God made it that way. Eden was perfect, and God was there. The whole world was perfect because it hadn't yet been spoiled by sin. When Adam and Eve sinned, God made them leave the Garden, and the whole world changed because of their sin. Thistles and thorns began to grow, animals began to eat each other, and human beings had to work hard at living in the world.

KEY VERSE: *So the Lord God sent him away from the Garden of Eden forever. He sent him out to farm the ground from which he had been taken. (Genesis 3:23)*

RELATED VERSES: *Genesis 3:17-19, 22-24; Isaiah 55:12-13; Romans 8:22*

RELATED QUESTIONS: *Why did Adam and Eve leave the Garden? Why wouldn't the angels let Adam and Eve into the Garden of Eden? Why were Adam and Eve naked?*

Q: WHY DID EVE DISOBEY GOD WHEN SHE KNEW SHE WOULD DIE?

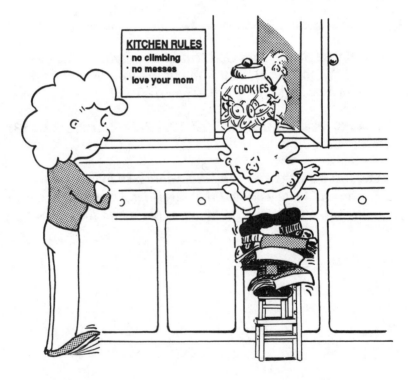

25

A: Eve disobeyed God because Satan *deceived* her. That is, the devil used lies and tricks to get her to disobey God. God had said that Adam and Eve would die if they ate of the "Tree of Conscience," but Satan said they wouldn't. Because Eve believed Satan, she wasn't sure what would happen. Another trick Satan used was to promise that it would do great things for her; he said that if she ate the forbidden fruit, she would be as God. That sounded good to Eve, and so she did what Satan suggested. Temptation tells you that feeling good right now is better than anything that might happen in the future. Satan still deceives people by twisting God's words and making people believe lies.

Satan wants us to think that once we sin, God can't forgive us. But even though Eve sinned, and even though we sin, God had a plan for taking away our sin. That plan was to send Jesus.

KEY VERSE: *"For you are the children of your father the devil. You love to do the evil things he does. He was a murderer from the beginning. There was no truth in him. When he lies, it is perfectly normal. For he is the father of lies."* *(John 8:44)*

RELATED VERSES: *Genesis 2:16-17; 3:1-5; Matthew 6:13; 26:41; 2 Corinthians 2:11*

RELATED QUESTIONS: *Did God want Eve to be deceived and eat of the fruit? Does God still love Adam and Eve?*

Q: WHY DID CAIN KILL
HIS BROTHER?

26

A: The story of Cain and Abel shows the effects of sin in the world. The first sin was when Adam and Eve disobeyed God and ate from the Tree of Conscience. After that, every person has been born a sinner, someone who will often do what's wrong instead of what's right. Cain's sins of jealousy and hatred led to murder. Both Cain and Abel had presented gifts to God, but Abel's gifts had pleased God, while Cain's had not. Cain became jealous of God's favor; this made Cain very angry (Genesis 4:5). Cain's jealousy and anger led him to kill his brother. We can see from this story that jealousy and anger can cause people to do terrible harm, even to people they love. Watch out for those feelings, and take care of them before they hurt you, too!

KEY VERSE: *We are not to be like Cain. He belonged to Satan and killed his brother. Why did he kill him? Because Cain had been doing wrong. He knew very well that his brother's life was better than his. (1 John 3:12)*

RELATED VERSES: *Genesis 4:1-16; Matthew 5:21-24; Hebrews 11:4*

RELATED QUESTION: *Why did Cain and Abel fight?*

HOW DID NOAH BUILD A BOAT THAT WAS SO BIG?

27

A: We don't know exactly *how* Noah built the huge boat (which we call the "ark"). But God told him what size to make it and what materials to use, and Noah obeyed God's instructions to the letter. The boat had to be very large because it would have to hold Noah, his children, their families, and hundreds of animals. It had to be a boat because God was going to flood the whole earth. It took a long time for Noah to build the boat. He probably used his whole family in the building project.

Why did Noah build the ark? Because everyone in the whole world had become so evil and violent, God was going to kill everyone with a flood. Noah was the only good man in the world, so he and his family would survive in the boat. And all the animals Noah brought on the ark would survive, too. Noah did everything God told him—he obeyed God.

KEY VERSE: *And Noah did all that God told him. (Genesis 6:22)*

RELATED VERSES: *Genesis 6:11-22; Hebrews 11:7*

RELATED QUESTIONS: *Why did Noah build a boat? Did God get into the ark before he shut the door? How did Noah get the animals from all over the earth? How did Noah gather all the animals on the ark?*

Q: WHY DID GOD FLOOD THE WHOLE EARTH?

28

A: God made the rain fall and the water rise in order to flood the whole earth so that all the evil people in the world would drown. Because of sin, the world had gotten worse and worse. It was so bad that God became very sad; God was even sorry that he had created human beings. People were evil, mean, cruel, and violent. God gave them 120 years to improve; they had many chances to obey God, but they only got worse. Only Noah and his family were trying to live God's way (only one family in the whole world!). Noah tried to tell people about God, but no one would listen. So God decided to destroy all the human beings, except Noah and his family.

KEY VERSE: *Meanwhile, the crime rate was rising rapidly across the earth. As seen by God, the world was rotten to the core. (Genesis 6:11)*

RELATED VERSES: *Genesis 6:11-13; Hebrews 11:7; 2 Peter 2:5*

RELATED QUESTIONS: *Why were all the other people bad? Was there not even one other Christian on the land anywhere in the world other than Noah? When the Flood came, did the people who could swim die too? Did fish die in the Flood?*

29

A: After the rains stopped, the flood waters went down, and Noah, his family, and the animals left the ark, God promised that he would never again send a flood to destroy the earth. Then God put a rainbow in the clouds as a sign of this promise. Whenever we see a rainbow, it reminds us of the Flood, the reason for it, and God's promise never to flood the earth again.

KEY VERSES: *"I will never again send another flood to destroy the earth. And I seal my promise with this sign. I have placed my rainbow in the clouds. It is a sign of my promise until the end of time, to you and to all the earth." (Genesis 9:11-13)*

RELATED VERSES: *Genesis 9:12-17*

RELATED QUESTIONS: *Did it ever rain before the Flood? Why did God give Noah a rainbow?*

NOTE TO PARENTS: *God gives us symbols and images to remind us of his love and promises. The cross, for example, reminds us of Christ's death for us. The empty tomb reminds us of his power over sin and death. His throne in heaven reminds us of his authority.*

Q: WHY DID GOD CHOOSE ABRAHAM TO GO TO THE PROMISED LAND INSTEAD OF SOMEONE ELSE?

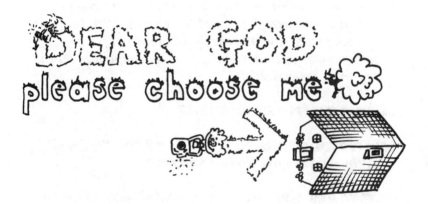

30

A: God chose Abraham (called Abram at first) to go to the Promised Land (which would later be called Israel) and to become the father of a great nation. Abraham was chosen, not because he was especially good, but simply because God wanted him—the Bible doesn't give us God's reasons. God doesn't always tell us why he does what he does. God knows everything and can do anything he wants. God knew that Abraham would obey.

KEY VERSES: *God had told Abram, "Leave your own country behind you, and your own people. Go to the land I will guide you to. If you do, I will cause you to become the father of a great nation. I will bless you and make your name famous. You will be a blessing to many others." (Genesis 12:1-2)*

RELATED VERSES: *Genesis 12:1-3; Hebrews 11:8-10*

RELATED QUESTIONS: *Why did God tell Abraham to go away from his home? Did God choose Abraham because he was the best person in the world?*

Q: WHY WAS ABRAHAM WILLING TO KILL HIS OWN SON?

31

A: One day God told Abraham to take his son, Isaac, up into the mountains and offer him as a sacrifice. Abraham took the trip and was willing to kill his own son because he knew that he had to obey God. Isaac was a miracle child, a special gift from God, and Abraham loved him very much. It was *very difficult* for Abraham to take Isaac and prepare him to be killed. But Abraham loved and obeyed God; he had faith and expected a miracle. Abraham believed that God could and would raise Isaac from the dead. This request from God was a test of Abraham's faith. Abraham believed that God's plan wouldn't be stopped. The good news, of course, is that Abraham didn't have to kill Isaac—God provided an animal to be sacrificed instead. Many years later, God sacrificed his own Son, Jesus, for us.

KEY VERSE: *[Abraham] believed that if Isaac died God would bring him back to life. That is just about what happened. As far as Abraham knew, Isaac was doomed to death. But he came back again, alive! (Hebrews 11:19)*

RELATED VERSES: *Genesis 22:1-19; Hebrews 11:17-19*

RELATED QUESTIONS: *If Abraham sacrificing his son was like God sacrificing Jesus, then why didn't God stop the people just before they killed Jesus? Why was it important for Abraham to have a son?*

Q: WHY DID JACOB TRICK HIS DAD?

32

A: Isaac had two sons, Jacob and Esau. Jacob tricked his father because he wanted the inheritance that should have gone to his brother. Jacob was selfish and greedy. Also, he was his mom's favorite child, and when his mother told him how to trick his father, he went along and did what she said. Although Jacob received the inheritance, his actions broke up the family and caused everyone a lot of grief.

KEY VERSES: *Rebekah: "Now do exactly as I tell you. Go out to the flocks and bring me two young goats. I will prepare your father's favorite dish from them. Then take it to your father. After he has enjoyed it he will bless you before his death, instead of Esau!" (Genesis 27:8-10)*

RELATED VERSES: *Genesis 27:1-40*

RELATED QUESTIONS: *Why did Jacob and Esau both want to be the leader? What's a birthright?*

WHY DID JOSEPH'S BROTHERS SELL HIM?

33

A: Joseph had ten older brothers (and one younger brother, Benjamin). Joseph's older brothers didn't like him because Joseph was their father's favorite son. (Joseph was Jacob's favorite because Joseph was born when Jacob was an old man.) They were jealous of him. Joseph's father even gave him a special gift—a beautiful coat. Joseph also made his brothers angry because he would tell his father about some of the bad things they would do, and he would tell his older brothers about his dreams in which the brothers bowed down before him. Eventually the brothers became so upset with Joseph that they decided to kill him. But one brother, Reuben, talked the others into putting Joseph into a well instead of killing him. He planned to set Joseph free later. But while Reuben was gone, the other brothers sold him to some foreign traders as a slave.

KEY VERSES: *"Here comes that master dreamer," they said. "Come on. Let's kill him and toss him into a well. We can tell Father that a wild animal has eaten him. Then we'll see what will become of all his dreams!" (Genesis 37:19-20)*

RELATED VERSES: *Genesis 37:12-36*

RELATED QUESTIONS: *Why did Joseph's dad give him a new coat? Why did Jacob love Joseph the best?*

Q: WHY DIDN'T JOSEPH GO BACK HOME?

34

A: Joseph may have wanted to go back home (certainly he missed his father, mother, and little brother), but he couldn't—first because he was a slave, then because he was in prison, and finally because he was in government service. He also was a long way from home, and transportation was different from today; Joseph couldn't just hop on a bus or train and go home. Also, Joseph may have been afraid of facing his brothers again; remember, they had wanted to kill him and then had sold him into slavery. It's good that Joseph stayed in Egypt because God used him in his powerful position in the government to save his family (and thousands of others) from starvation. And eventually God brought the whole family back together again in Egypt with Joseph—all part of God's plan to bring Jesus to earth.

KEY VERSE: *"Yes, it was God who sent me here, not you! And he has made me a counselor to Pharaoh. I am the manager of this entire nation, ruler of all the land of Egypt." (Genesis 45:8)*

RELATED VERSES: *Genesis 41:41-57; 45:4-9*

RELATED QUESTION: *When Joseph's brothers came back to Egypt to live with him, why did they think he was still mad at them?*

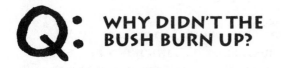

Q: WHY DIDN'T THE BUSH BURN UP?

35

A: One day while watching sheep, a man named Moses saw a bush on fire that would not burn up. The bush didn't turn into ashes because God was present, doing a miracle to get Moses' attention. When Moses saw the bush and heard God's voice, he was ready to listen. God used the burning bush to help Moses see that God had the power to do what he said he would do—rescue the people of Israel from slavery in Egypt.

KEY VERSES: *Suddenly the Angel of the Lord appeared to [Moses] as a flame of fire in a bush. Moses saw that the bush was on fire. But it didn't burn up. So he went over to see why. Then God called out to him, "Moses! Moses!" "Who is it?" Moses asked. (Exodus 3:2-4)*

RELATED VERSES: *Exodus 3:1–4:18*

RELATED QUESTIONS: *How did God choose Moses? Did God know that Moses would be afraid to go? Was Jesus in the burning bush? How did Moses make his shepherd rod into a snake?*

Q: WHY WASN'T MOSES AFRAID TO GO TO PHARAOH?

36

A: Moses probably was afraid to go to Pharaoh, but he went anyway out of obedience to God. When God said he was going to send Moses to Pharaoh to demand that he let the Israelites go, Moses was very frightened at the idea. In fact, he tried to get out of the job by using all sorts of excuses: he said he wasn't the right person, the people would wonder why he should be the one to lead them, the people wouldn't believe that God had sent him, and he wasn't a good speaker. Finally, when Moses had run out of excuses, he simply pleaded: "Lord, please! Send someone else" (Exodus 4:13). But God wanted Moses to go, and Moses did go—God gave him strength and stayed with him. Moses was able to lead God's people out of slavery and to the Promised Land. The Bible doesn't say Moses wasn't afraid; it says he obeyed God.

KEY VERSE: *"Now I am going to send you to Pharaoh. You will demand that he let you lead my people out of Egypt."* *(Exodus 3:10)*

RELATED VERSES: *Exodus 3:7–4:17*

RELATED QUESTIONS: *Why were all the Israelites slaves except for Moses? Why would God let the magicians do the same miracles as Aaron and Moses? How did the sorcerers do the same miracles as Moses? How come Moses kept asking God to take away the plagues when he knew Pharaoh would change his mind again?*

Q: WHY WOULDN'T PHARAOH LET THE PEOPLE GO?

37

A: Pharaoh is a title, like "king." The pharaoh in charge of Egypt when Moses lived was different from the pharaoh whom Joseph served—that pharaoh was kind and generous to the Israelites. But this pharaoh was mean; he forced the Israelites to serve the Egyptians as slaves. When Moses went to see Pharaoh and asked him to let the Israelites leave Egypt to worship in the wilderness, Pharaoh was furious. He was too proud to give in to a slave, and he thought he would lose his slave labor, so he refused. Moses went back to him with the request and did special signs to prove that he had been sent by God, but Pharaoh still said no. Finally God sent a series of plagues to convince Pharaoh to let the people go. After each plague, Pharaoh would agree to let the people go, but then he would change his mind and refuse. The Lord hardened Pharaoh's heart in order to punish him and demonstrate God's power.

KEY VERSE: *"This is the finger of God," [the magicians] exclaimed to Pharaoh. But Pharaoh's heart was hard and stubborn. He wouldn't listen to them, just as the Lord had predicted. (Exodus 8:19)*

RELATED VERSES: *Exodus 5:1-9; 6:1-13; 7:1-14; 8:1–12:36*

RELATED QUESTIONS: *Why did the Lord keep hardening Pharaoh's heart? Was the pharaoh who wouldn't let the Israelites go the same one that Joseph knew?*

Q: WHY DID GOD SEND PLAGUES ON EGYPT?

38

A: God sent the plagues to Egypt to punish Pharaoh and to show God's power. The plagues were miracles—fantastic demonstrations of God's power. Pharaoh saw himself as a god, and God was showing him who the true God was. Also, God was answering the prayers of the Israelites to deliver them from slavery. The Egyptians were holding the Israelites captive and did not want to let them go. Each time Pharaoh would refuse to let the people go, God would send a plague on the Egyptians (but not the Israelites) to help convince Pharaoh to change his mind. After each plague, Pharaoh would agree to release the Israelites, but then he would harden his heart and say no. Eventually, after the death of the firstborn male children, the Israelites were allowed to leave Egypt. But even then, Pharaoh changed his mind and chased after them. Pharaoh was an evil man.

KEY VERSES: *"Go back to Pharaoh," the Lord told Moses. "Tell him, 'The Lord . . . demands that you let his people go to sacrifice to him. If you refuse, the power of God will send a deadly plague. It will destroy your cattle, horses, donkeys, camels, flocks, and herds. But the plague will affect only the cattle of Egypt. None of the Israelite herds and flocks will even be touched!'" (Exodus 9:1-4)*

RELATED VERSES: *Exodus 3:5-10; 7:14–12:33*

RELATED QUESTIONS: *Did the hail fall on the Israelites? How can darkness be felt? How could it be dark in one place and light in another? Why did Pharaoh want the Israelites to come back? Did Pharaoh get the boils as well? Did the Egyptians slaves get killed in the hail? How could the Nile river being blood have fresh water around to dig up?*

Q: WHY DID THE ISRAELITES
SMEAR BLOOD ON
THEIR DOORS?

39

A: The blood on the doors helped the Israelites prepare for God's final plague on Egypt. That plague would kill all the firstborn males in Egypt except those who lived in the homes marked by the blood on the doors. The blood came from a perfect lamb that they killed and ate that night. The blood showed their faith that God would do as he said and rescue them from slavery. Though the people at that time didn't know it, the blood also represented Christ's death on the cross. By trusting in Jesus, men and women and boys and girls can be rescued from slavery to sin . . . and receive *eternal* life.

KEY VERSE: *"For the Lord will pass through the land and kill the Egyptians. But he will see the blood on the panel at the top of the door and on the two side pieces. And he will pass over that home. He will not permit the Destroyer to enter and kill your firstborn." (Exodus 12:23)*

RELATED VERSES: *Exodus 12:1-36; Hebrews 11:28*

RELATED QUESTIONS: *Why did God kill the Egyptian babies? What did the Israelites take with them when they left Egypt? How come the Israelites couldn't cook their bread before they left Egypt? How come the Israelites couldn't have any lamb leftovers?*

NOTE TO PARENTS: *It is sometimes difficult for children to understand why God asked his people to sacrifice animals. Explain that God does everything for our good—God is love, and he does whatever benefits us all. He's just and kind, and his plans for us are good.*

Q: HOW DID MOSES PART THE RED SEA?

40

A: After Moses and the Israelites left Egypt, Pharaoh changed his mind and sent soldiers to bring them back. When the fleeing Israelites came to the Red Sea, it looked as if they would be caught by the soldiers because there seemed to be no way across the water. But Moses held his rod over the edge of the sea, and God made the waters part so the people could march across to the other side on dry ground. Moses himself didn't part the Red Sea—it was a miracle that God did through him. God used Moses to lead the people to safety. Once the Israelites were safe on the other side, God allowed the water to return to normal, and the Egyptian army was drowned.

KEY VERSES: *Meanwhile, Moses stretched his rod over the sea. The Lord opened up a path through the sea. There were walls of water on each side. And a strong east wind blew all that night. It dried the sea bottom. So the people of Israel walked through the sea on dry ground! (Exodus 14:21-22)*

RELATED VERSES: *Exodus 14:15-31; Hebrews 11:29*

RELATED QUESTIONS: *How did God part the Red Sea? How could God make the wheels of the chariots fall off? Why did Pharaoh want the Israelites to come back?*

Q: WHY DID GOD GIVE MOSES SO MANY LAWS FOR THE ISRAELITES TO OBEY?

41

A: Moses led the Israelites to Mount Sinai, where God met with Moses and gave him laws that are recorded in the book of Leviticus. When we read Leviticus, it seems as if God gave the Israelites a lot of laws to obey. Actually, today most cities and towns have far more laws than are listed in Leviticus. (The basic laws are the Ten Commandments—many of the other laws grew out of these.) Some of the laws God gave helped organize the Israelites into a nation; some helped keep the people healthy; others told them (and us) how to live. God knew what was best for the people, and he wanted what was best for them, so he gave them many instructions.

KEY VERSE: *Moses kept on speaking to the people of Israel. He said, "Listen carefully now to all these laws God has given you. Learn them, and be sure to obey them!" (Deuteronomy 5:1)*

RELATED VERSES: *Exodus 20:1-17; Deuteronomy 5:1-22; Galatians 3:24*

RELATED QUESTIONS: *Why did God give Moses only ten commandments? Why didn't the rest of the Israelites go up the mountain with Moses and talk to God?*

NOTE TO PARENTS: *The law guided the Israelites, but it also shows us that we are sinners. That is, it shows us that we can't obey perfectly. You can use this to explain how we all break God's law, making us guilty before God and in need of salvation through faith in Christ.*

Q: WHY DID THE ISRAELITES WHO LEFT EGYPT HAVE TO WANDER IN THE WILDERNESS UNTIL THEY DIED?

42

A: Through Moses, God led the Israelites right to the Promised Land, the land he had promised to Abraham. (This is also the land that Jacob and his sons left when they went to live with Joseph in Egypt.) Moses had sent twelve spies into Canaan to see what the land and the Canaanites were like. Ten spies reported that the Canaanites were giants that the Israelites shouldn't try to fight. But Joshua and Caleb, who knew God would help them, said, "Let us go up at once and possess it! For we are well able to conquer it!" (Numbers 13:30). Unfortunately, the people listened to the report of the ten and refused to obey God and march into the land. Those Israelites never saw the Promised Land because they didn't have faith to do what God wanted them to do; they wandered in the wilderness for forty years.

KEY VERSES: *"'The spies were in the land for 40 days. Thus, you must wander in the wilderness for 40 years. You will wander a year for each day. You will bear the burden of your sins. I will teach you what it means to reject me. I, the Lord, have spoken. Every one of you who has turned against me shall die here in this wilderness.'" (Numbers 14:34-35)*

RELATED VERSES: *Numbers 13:1–14:45*

RELATED QUESTIONS: *Why did the Israelites listen to the ten unbelieving spies instead of to Joshua and Caleb? Why did Joshua only send two spies into the Promised Land instead of twelve? Why did the Israelites believe they could go into the Promised Land the second time when they didn't believe the first time?*

Q: DID THE ISRAELITES HAVE LAWYERS AND COURTS FOR THEIR JUDGES?

43

A: Joshua was the Israelites' leader when they first got to the Promised Land. After Joshua died, God used judges to lead his people. The judges that we read about in the book of Judges were not like the judges we have today, so they didn't have courts or listen to lawyers. The Israelite judges were their nation's spiritual leaders and sometimes military leaders. Their main job was to organize the people, rescue them from enemies, and lead the people to God. This was how God led the Israelites, much the way parents lead their children.

KEY VERSE: *The Lord raised up judges. They were chosen to save the Israelites from their enemies. (Judges 2:16)*

RELATED VERSES: *Judges 2:16-23; 1 Samuel 8:1-22*

RELATED QUESTION: *What is a judge?*

Q: WAS SAMSON A GOOD GUY OR A BAD GUY?

44

A: One of Israel's judges was a man named Samson. Samson served God and wanted to please him, but he wasn't perfect. God had chosen him to do a special service for the nation of Israel—to rescue his people from cruel enemies. Samson fulfilled that job well. But Samson also did some cruel and foolish things, just as most people do. God didn't force him to do everything right. Like us, Samson had the freedom to choose to use his God-given abilities (in his case, strength) for good or bad. Sometimes Samson chose to go his own way instead of God's.

KEY VERSE: *"Your son's hair must never be cut. For he shall be a Nazirite. He shall be a special servant of God from the day he is born. And he will begin to rescue Israel from the Philistines." (Judges 13:5)*

RELATED VERSES: *Judges 13:1–16:31*

RELATED QUESTION: *Why did the Philistines want to capture Samson?*

Q: WHY DID SAMSON TELL DELILAH HIS SECRET?

45

A: Samson was in love with a woman named Delilah even though Delilah did not really love him and was a friend of his enemies. When some of those enemies offered her money to help them capture Samson, Delilah agreed and asked him for the secret of his strength. At first he gave her the wrong answers, but she nagged him and prodded him until finally Samson told her the truth—his strength came from God as part of a vow that included not cutting his hair. He told her that if his hair were cut, the Lord and his strength would leave him. Samson let himself be tricked because he was blinded by his feelings for Delilah. We need to be careful about our friends; even people we care about and like may sometimes want us to do bad things. Whenever that happens, we should obey God.

KEY VERSES: *She nagged at him every day until he couldn't stand it any longer. In the end, he told her his secret. "My hair has never been cut," he confessed. "For I've been a Nazirite to God since before my birth. If my hair were cut, my strength would leave me. I would become as weak as anyone else." (Judges 16:16-17)*

RELATED VERSES: *Judges 16:1-22*

RELATED QUESTIONS: *How did Samson get his strength? When Delilah kept asking Samson about what his secret was, why did he tell her when he knew she would tell the Philistines?*

Q: WHY DID HANNAH LEAVE HER SON AT THE CHURCH?

46

A: For a long time, Hannah was unable to have children, and that bothered her very much. One day, while crying and praying to God, she vowed that if God would answer her prayer and give her a son, she would give the boy back to God, dedicating his life to serving God. When Samuel was born, Hannah remembered her promise to God; a few years later, when Samuel was old enough to eat solid food, she brought Samuel to the tabernacle (the place where God's people worshiped). Leaving Samuel there was like leaving him at a boarding school, with people who would love and care for him and teach him God's ways. Hannah wasn't abandoning Samuel; she was leaving him with teachers who would train him to become a priest and servant of God. Hannah's son was in good hands. Samuel grew up to be a leader of Israel and a spokesman for God.

KEY VERSES: *"I asked [God] to give me this child. And he has given me what I asked for! Now I am giving him to the Lord for as long as he lives." So [Hannah] left him there at the Tabernacle for the Lord to use. (1 Samuel 1:27-28)*

RELATED VERSES: *1 Samuel 1:1-28; 2:20-21*

RELATED QUESTION: *Why did God choose Samuel instead of a grown-up or someone who knew him better?*

NOTE TO PARENTS: *Questions like this one may have others hidden underneath: Will I be left alone with strangers? Does God think it's good for children to be left with strangers? Do my parents care about me? Be sensitive to this concern and reassure your children of God's care and your commitment to love and nurture them.*

47

A: The people of Israel were unhappy with God as their king and wanted to be like all the other nations—to have a human king who would lead them in battle. Times were tough, and Samuel's sons were turning out to be bad judges. They were accepting bribes and making wrong decisions. Samuel knew that God wanted the people to trust in God and not in a king, but God told Samuel to give them one anyway, along with a warning that a king would bring them many hardships. The man chosen to be Israel's first king was Saul; he was tall and handsome, but very shy. Saul started out to be a good king, but then became bad because he disobeyed God.

KEY VERSE: *"Do as they say," the Lord replied. "For I am the one they are rejecting, not you. They do not want me to be their king any longer." (1 Samuel 8:7)*

RELATED VERSES: *1 Samuel 8:1-22*

RELATED QUESTIONS: *Why did Saul hide in the baggage? Was Saul a wicked man?*

Q: WHAT DID GOLIATH EAT THAT MADE HIM SO BIG?

48

A: Goliath was a very big man—over nine feet tall. If he were alive today, he would be able to dunk a basketball without jumping, and his head would touch the net. We don't know how Goliath got to be so big, but he was a giant of a man. Goliath was as nasty as he was big; he hated the Israelites and would make fun of them and God. King Saul and his soldiers were afraid of fighting him. But a young man named David wasn't afraid. He knew that he had to fight against this man who stood against God, no matter how big he was. And he knew he would win because God would fight for him.

KEY VERSE: *Then Goliath came out of the Philistine ranks to face Israel's army. He was a Philistine champion from Gath. Goliath was a giant of a man! He was over nine feet tall! (1 Samuel 17:4)*

RELATED VERSES: *1 Samuel 17:4-11*

RELATED QUESTIONS: *How tall was Goliath? How did Goliath get so tall if his mom was a regular-sized person? Was Goliath's mom a giant? How did Goliath get so big?*

Q: HOW DID DAVID FIGHT
GOLIATH IF HE WAS SO SMALL?

49

A: Although David wasn't a big man or a soldier, he wasn't afraid to fight the giant Goliath because he trusted in God, not in his own strength or in a soldier's weapons and armor. In fact, he wouldn't wear the king's armor when it was offered to him. David remembered that he had defeated lions and bears while protecting his father's sheep. David also knew that he would not fight Goliath in hand-to-hand combat; instead, he would use a sling and a stone. Also, David was about sixteen, not a little boy. David trusted in God and knew that he had to fight Goliath because Goliath was mocking the armies of Israel and God.

KEY VERSE: *David shouted in reply, "You come to me with a sword and spear. But I come to you in the name of the Lord of the armies of heaven and of Israel. I come in the name of the God whom you have defied." (1 Samuel 17:45)*

RELATED VERSES: *1 Samuel 17:12-58*

RELATED QUESTIONS: *Why did King Saul put heavy armor on David? Why wasn't David afraid of Goliath? How could David as a little boy fight a big, big giant? Why did the Philistines turn and run when David killed Goliath? How come David took Goliath's head with him?*

Q: WHY WAS SAUL JEALOUS OF DAVID?

50

A: After Saul made David an army commander, people were singing, "Saul has killed his thousands, and David his ten thousands!" (1 Samuel 18:7). It angered Saul that David had become so popular with the people; in fact, it seemed as though everyone liked David more than Saul. This made Saul jealous. Saul knew that David was a better man—a better warrior and a better person. This jealousy made Saul a very cruel and deceitful person, and he tried for years to kill David. Eventually God told Saul he couldn't be king anymore, and after Saul died, David became king. We must be careful to be content with whom God has made us and not become jealous of others.

KEY VERSES: *Of course, Saul was very angry. "What's this?" he said to himself. "They credit David with ten thousands and me with only thousands. Next they'll be making him their king!" So from that time on King Saul was jealous of David. (1 Samuel 18:8-9)*

RELATED VERSES: *1 Samuel 18:6-9*

RELATED QUESTIONS: *Why did Saul throw his spear at Jonathan? Why did an evil spirit come on Saul from God? Why would Saul want to kill David when he is married to his daughter Michal?*

Q: WHY DID SOLOMON WANT TO CUT THE BABY IN HALF?

51

A: After David died, his son Solomon became king. God told Solomon that he could have anything he asked for. Solomon asked for wisdom. One day two women came to King Solomon arguing over who was the real mother of a baby, and Solomon suggested that he cut the baby in half and give one half to each mother. Solomon didn't want to kill the baby. He just suggested that they cut the baby in half in order to find out who was the baby's real mother. Solomon knew that the real mother would never let such a thing happen to her baby. Solomon's trick worked, and the baby was given to his real mother. This story is in the Bible to show how wise Solomon was, in answer to his prayer. God made him the wisest man who ever lived.

KEY VERSES: *So [God] replied, "You did not ask for a long life. You did not ask for riches for yourself. You did not ask me to defeat your enemies. Instead, you asked for wisdom in ruling my people. Yes, I'll give you what you asked for! I will make you wiser than anyone else ever has been or will be!" (1 Kings 3:11-12)*

RELATED VERSES: *1 Kings 3:3-28*

RELATED QUESTIONS: *Why did God make Solomon rich when he only asked for wisdom? How did Solomon get to be so smart?*

Q: WERE PROPHETS THE PEOPLE IN BIBLE DAYS WHO MADE LOTS OF MONEY?

52

A: It's easy to confuse words that sound alike but have different meanings. *Profit* refers to making money; *prophet* means a person who represented God to the people in Bible times. A prophet spoke God's messages and told the people to obey God. People never became prophets in order to become rich or famous. Most of the time—especially when they had to give bad news—prophets were very unpopular; some were even put in prison. But God's prophets were willing to risk everything for God. Some of the most famous prophets include Moses, Elijah, Elisha, Isaiah, Jeremiah, Ezekiel, and Daniel. Some less well-known prophets also wrote books of the Bible: Hosea, Joel, Amos, Obadiah, Jonah, and Malachi. Even though these prophets spoke hundreds of years ago, their messages apply to us, too, and we should listen to what they had to say.

KEY VERSE: *Long ago God spoke in many different ways to our fathers. He spoke through the prophets in visions, dreams, and even face to face. Little by little he told them about his plans. (Hebrews 1:1)*

RELATED VERSES: *Deuteronomy 18:15-22; Jeremiah 1:5; Ezekiel 2:5; 2 Peter 1:20-21*

RELATED QUESTIONS: *What does **prophet** mean? What does a prophet do?*

NOTE TO PARENTS: *Many children think prophets mainly foretold the future. But their main job was to "forth-tell" God's word to the people, to challenge the people to turn back to God. Often the prophets' messages contained predictions about the future, but most of the messages were calls or challenges to obey God and live right.*

Q: WHY DID ELIJAH GO UP TO HEAVEN SO EARLY?

53

A: Elijah was a famous prophet who spent most of his life telling others about God. He is one of only two people mentioned in the Bible who didn't die before going to heaven (Enoch is the other one—see Genesis 5:21-24). Instead, God took them. God used a chariot of fire and a whirlwind to take Elijah to heaven. The whirlwind and fire didn't kill Elijah or burn him; rather, the chariot and horses separated Elijah from his good friend and student, Elisha. Then the whirlwind carried Elijah to heaven. This showed that God approved of Elijah and that Elijah was a good man who loved God. And God took Elijah to heaven at just the right time, not early. We don't know how old Elijah was when God took him; he may have been an old man.

KEY VERSE: *[Elijah and Elisha] were walking along, talking. Then suddenly a chariot of fire came. It was pulled by horses of fire. It drove between them and separated them. Then Elijah was carried by a whirlwind into heaven. (2 Kings 2:11)*

RELATED VERSES: *2 Kings 2:1-12; Matthew 16:14; 17:3; 27:49; James 5:17*

RELATED QUESTIONS: *Why would God want to bring Elijah to heaven? Why was the chariot on fire?*

NOTE TO PARENTS: *Children often imagine that the chariot of fire would have killed Elijah and burned Elisha because it was on fire. We don't know what the "fire" was like. The point of the image is that God used a dramatic and miraculous event to separate Elijah and Elisha and to take Elijah to heaven.*

Q: WHY DID GOD SEND THE JEWS TO BABYLON?

54

A: The people of Judah (the Jews) didn't listen to the prophets. They turned away from God, worshiped idols, and mistreated the poor. So God allowed a wicked nation, Babylon, and a wicked king, Nebuchadnezzar, to capture their cities and take many of the people to Babylon. The Babylonians often did this to the people they conquered; they removed the best young people from their own country and trained them in Babylonian ways. Prophets like Jeremiah predicted that this would happen, and they were very sad about it. The Jews spent seventy years in Babylon, just as God said they would. God's warnings are for our good. When we ignore them again and again, we end up being hurt, just like the people of Judah did.

KEY VERSE: *King Nebuchadnezzar took 10,000 captives from Jerusalem. This included all the princes. It also included the best of the soldiers, craftsmen, and smiths. So only the poorest and least skilled people were left in the land. (2 Kings 24:14)*

RELATED VERSES: *2 Kings 20:17; 24:1–25:24; Jeremiah 34:1-22; Ezekiel 7:1-4; 8:17-18; 14:22*

RELATED QUESTIONS: *Why did God get a wicked king to take over Jerusalem and capture the people? Why did Jeremiah write a sad book?*

NOTE TO PARENTS: *The Babylonian captivity came as a result of Israel's failure to heed the prophets. It shows God's willingness to discipline his people for their own good. In Judah's case, the time in Babylon taught them not to worship idols anymore.*

WHOSE HAND MADE THE WRITING ON THE WALL?

55

A: It was a miracle of God, performed to announce judgment on the king of Babylon for his pride. Belshazzar was holding a great feast and serving a lot of wine. During the eating and drinking, he sent for the gold and silver cups that had been taken from the temple in Jerusalem many years before by a king who ruled before him, King Nebuchadnezzar. As he was using these cups to drink a toast to idols of wood and stone, fingers of a man's hand appeared and began writing on the wall. The king was shocked and frightened, and he called for Daniel (one of God's prophets) to interpret the writing. It contained a message for the king: He had been evil and proud, and soon his enemies would defeat him (which they did). God used the hand and the writing to get the king's attention, and it certainly worked!

KEY VERSES: *They were drinking from these cups when suddenly they saw the fingers of a man's hand. The hand was writing on the plaster of the wall across from the lampstand. The king himself saw the fingers as they wrote. He was so afraid that his knees knocked together. His legs began to give way under him. (Daniel 5:5-6)*

RELATED VERSES: *Proverbs 18:12; Daniel 5:1-31*

RELATED QUESTION: *Why did God write on the wall?*

HOW DID DANIEL SLEEP WITH THE LIONS WITHOUT BEING AFRAID?

56

A: Daniel was a young man when he was captured and taken to Babylon. He lived the rest of his life there, serving four kings, but he always remained true to God. One day, when he was an old man, the last of these kings, Darius, signed a law stating that no one could ask a favor of (or pray to) anyone except him, the king. (This was a trick by some powerful men to get rid of Daniel.) Because Daniel ignored the new law and continued to pray to God, the king had to punish him by putting him into a den of lions. Daniel spent all night with the lions but wasn't hurt.

The Bible doesn't say that Daniel wasn't afraid. Rather, Daniel was willing to face the lions because he trusted in God. Daniel had seen what God could do (see Daniel 3:1-30 and 5:1-31) and believed that obeying God was right, even if it meant being in danger. Even if Daniel was afraid, he faced the lions *bravely* because of his confidence in God.

KEY VERSE: *"My God has sent his angel. He shut the lions' mouths so that they can't touch me. I am innocent before God. And I have not done anything wrong to you."* *(Daniel 6:22)*

RELATED VERSES: *Psalms 3:6; 23:4; 27:1; 91:5; Daniel 6:1-28*

RELATED QUESTIONS: *Why did they want to throw Daniel in the lions' den? What would have happened if Daniel had obeyed Darius and didn't pray three times a day anymore?*

WHY DIDN'T THE JEWS EVER CHANGE THEIR CLOTHES WHILE THEY WERE REBUILDING THE WALLS?

57

A: After seventy years in Babylon, God had the king begin to let his people go back home again. Although Nehemiah lived in Babylon and served the king there, he still loved his own country, Israel, especially the capital city, Jerusalem. When he heard that the walls were still torn down, he became very upset. (In those days, a city's walls helped protect it from invading armies, and good, solid walls showed that the city was doing well.) So Nehemiah asked for and received permission from the king to return to Jerusalem to organize the wall-building project. Not everyone in Jerusalem and the surrounding areas wanted the wall to be rebuilt; some were trying hard to stop the project. So all the workers had to be on guard constantly and to be organized so that the work could continue twenty-four hours a day. Nehemiah and the workers were so determined to rebuild the walls that they didn't change their clothes (except to wash) and always kept their weapons with them. Soon the wall was rebuilt.

KEY VERSE: *During this time we never took off our clothes except for washing. This included me, my brothers, the servants, and the guards who were with me. And we carried our weapons with us at all times. (Nehemiah 4:23)*

RELATED VERSES: *Nehemiah 1:1–2:20; 4:1-23*

RELATED QUESTIONS: *Why didn't all the Jews go back to Israel? Why did Nehemiah cry when he heard that the walls of Jerusalem were broken? Why didn't the Jews rebuild the walls of Jerusalem before Nehemiah came?*

Q: WHAT'S A MACCABEE?

58

A: The Maccabees were a courageous and heroic family of Jews who lived between the time of the Old and New Testaments. The events in the Old Testament ended about four hundred years before the events in the New Testament began. But during that time, Israel was still ruled by other nations, and most of the rulers were cruel to them. One ruler from Greece even made fun of the Jewish religion by sacrificing a pig in the temple. This greatly upset the Jews, and so they rebelled. The revolt was led by Judas Maccabee (who, by the way, was no relation to the Judas who betrayed Jesus). Under his leadership, the Jews were able to win many battles and eventually restore the temple to the way it was. They celebrated with a great festival, which came to be called Hanukkah, or the "Feast of Lights" (referred to as the "Feast of Dedication" in the New Testament). It became an annual event, beginning in December and lasting eight days.

KEY VERSE: *It was winter. Jesus was in Jerusalem for the Feast of Dedication. (John 10:22)*

RELATED QUESTIONS: *Why doesn't the Bible tell us about the four hundred years before the New Testament? What happened between the Old and New Testaments?*

NEW
TESTAMENT
EVENTS
AND
PEOPLE

Q: WHY WAS JESUS BORN IN A STINKY STABLE?

59

A: God sent his own Son, Jesus, when the time was right. Jesus' birth tells us the kind of Savior he is. At the time Jesus was born, the Roman ruler of Palestine (where the Jews lived—Israel's Promised Land) was Herod, an evil man. Herod had great forts and palaces built so he could feel safe and powerful. One of the huge forts was right outside Bethlehem. But Jesus—the *true king* and ruler of the universe—came to earth and was born in a stinky stable. Herod's kingdom and power were very temporary; he's dead and his buildings are in ruins. But Jesus' kingdom and power last forever. So one reason Jesus was born in such a place was to show us that he and his ways are the opposite of the world's. Jesus' kingdom doesn't come by force but by God working in each person. Jesus' birth in a stable also lets us know that he came for *all* people, not just the rich and famous.

KEY VERSES: *And while [Joseph and Mary] were there, the time came for her baby to be born. So she gave birth to her first child, a son. She wrapped him in a blanket and laid him in a manger. This was because there was no room for them in the village inn. (Luke 2:6-7)*

RELATED VERSES: *Luke 2:1-7, 11-12; Philippians 2:5-7*

RELATED QUESTIONS: *Did Mary have other babies, too? How could Mary have her baby without going to the hospital?*

NOTE TO PARENTS: *Children may ask the related question, "How could Mary have a baby if she wasn't married to God?" The best answer is, "I don't know." Exactly how Mary conceived is a mystery. Jesus was unique—the only Son of God. Jesus' birth was a miracle.*

NEW TESTAMENT EVENTS AND PEOPLE

Q: DID PEOPLE IN THE BIBLE HAVE CHRISTMAS?

60

A: Christmas is a celebration of the birth of Christ. Many years after Jesus was born, Christians decided to celebrate his birth. They chose December 25 as the day to observe it. December 25 is probably not the exact day Jesus was born, but that's not important. What is important is that we remember and celebrate the birth of Jesus, our Savior, not that we get presents, get time off from school, or get to eat a lot of sweets.

KEY VERSE: *Jesus was born in the town of Bethlehem, in Judea. He was born during the reign of King Herod. (Matthew 2:1)*

RELATED VERSES: *Isaiah 9:6-7; 16:5; Micah 5:2; Matthew 1:18–2:11; Luke 2:1-20*

RELATED QUESTIONS: *When was Christmas made? Was Jesus really born on Christmas? Why isn't Santa Claus in the Bible?*

NOTE TO PARENTS: *If your children ask about Santa Claus, explain that he was a person whom people have used to help celebrate Christmas. Many years ago, the real St. Nicholas was a man who helped poor children at Christmas time by giving them gifts. Since that time, the story has grown so that today we talk about Santa Claus, with his flying reindeer, who delivers presents to children all over the world. Santa isn't real, but Jesus is.*

Q: WHY DO ANGELS LIGHT UP AND GET BRIGHT?

61

A: When the angels came to tell about Jesus'
birth, they glowed brightly. But angels don't
always appear that way. When angels appeared to
Abraham, for example, he thought they were ordinary
men and offered them an evening meal (see Genesis
18:1-5). Angels may become bright to reflect God and
his glory, or just whenever it is necessary, such as at
night (which was when the angels appeared to the
shepherds). As God's messengers, it's only fitting that
they would light up and get bright because that's how it
is in heaven, where they stand with God: "And the city
has no need of sun or moon to light it. The glory of God
and of the Lamb give it light" (Revelation 21:23).

KEY VERSE: *Suddenly an angel was there with them! And the
hills shone bright with the glory of the Lord. They were
very afraid. (Luke 2:9)*

RELATED VERSES: *Genesis 19:1; Exodus 3:2; Judges 13:6,
15, 20; Luke 1:11-20; 2:9-13*

RELATED QUESTION: *Why were shepherds afraid of angels?*

NOTE TO PARENTS: *People have many ideas about angels.
Some think angels made regular appearances to biblical
folks; in fact, they rarely did. Some think of angels as
men with wings, yet many accounts don't mention wings.
Some people speak of guardian angels, but the Bible
describes angels as God's messengers, not our guardians.
And some think too much of angels; Samson's parents
tried to worship an angel and were told not to, and
Hebrews 1 reminds us that Christ is superior to any
angel. Your children may have different ideas about
angels. Remember to look to God's Word for the truth.*

Q: HOW COME ZACHARIAS COULDN'T TALK UNTIL HIS SON WAS BORN?

62

A: Zacharias was a priest who served in the temple. One day he entered a part of the sanctuary where only the priest could go. There the angel Gabriel appeared to him and announced that Zacharias's wife, Elizabeth, would have a son. Zacharias doubted the angel's promise, and so he was silenced until the birth of the baby. This would be a sign to the people that Zacharias had met with God. When Zacharias's son was born, he asked for a writing tablet to write down the boy's name. As soon as he wrote, "His name is John!" as Gabriel had told him to do, Zacharias was able to talk again.

KEY VERSE: *When he finally came out, he couldn't speak to them. But they saw from his motions that he must have seen a vision in the Temple. (Luke 1:22)*

RELATED VERSES: *Luke 1:5-23, 57-63*

RELATED QUESTIONS: *What month was John the Baptist born? How come Zacharias asked for a writing tablet?*

Q: WHY DID JOHN THE BAPTIST LIVE IN THE DESERT?

63

A: John the Baptist was a prophet. God had given him the important job of preparing the way for Jesus. So John wanted to preach away from where people were living so they would have to go out to see him and hear his message. Living in the desert also kept him from having a lot of arguments with the religious leaders in Jerusalem who didn't like what he was saying. And by living in the desert, John was showing that he was serious about his message and that a person's relationship with God was much more important than having a nice, comfortable life on earth.

KEY VERSES: *While [Mary, Joseph, and Jesus] were living in Nazareth, John the Baptist began preaching in the Judean desert. He said, "Turn from your sins! Turn to God! For the Kingdom of Heaven is coming soon." (Matthew 3:1-2)*

RELATED VERSES: *Isaiah 40:3; Matthew 3:1-17; John 1:19-34*

RELATED QUESTION: *Why didn't Herod want to kill John the Baptist?*

WHY DID THE HOLY SPIRIT COME DOWN ON JESUS LIKE A DOVE?

64

A: When Jesus was thirty years old, John the Baptist baptized him. When Jesus came up out of the water, the Holy Spirit came down on him in the form of a dove. The Holy Spirit is a spirit and doesn't have a body, so the Spirit took a form that people could see. A dove was a great form to take because when people saw doves, they thought of peace and purity, and that's exactly what the Holy Spirit brings to people. After Jesus left the earth, he sent the Holy Spirit to live here in his place. But now, instead of taking a special form, the Holy Spirit lives inside us. When a person trusts in Christ as Savior, the Holy Spirit comes to live inside him or her.

KEY VERSE: *The Holy Spirit settled upon [Jesus] in the form of a dove. And a voice from Heaven said, "You are my much-loved Son. Yes, you are my delight." (Luke 3:22)*

RELATED VERSES: *Matthew 3:16; Mark 1:10; John 1:32*

RELATED QUESTIONS: *What does the Holy Spirit look like? Where is the Holy Spirit today?*

Q: HOW DID JESUS DO MIRACLES?

65

A: Jesus was able to do miracles because he was God's Son. The miracles weren't magic or tricks; they really happened. Jesus performed miracles because he had compassion on people and because he wanted to show the people that he was the Messiah, the promised one from God. Only God can do real miracles. Sometimes God worked his miracles through special people, like the prophets or apostles. We read in the Bible about a lot of miracles, but miracles didn't happen every day. More miracles happened when Jesus was on earth than at any other time, but only during the three years that he was preaching and teaching in public. Jesus didn't do miracles to show off, and he didn't heal everybody. He had a purpose for everything he did.

KEY VERSES: *Jesus' disciples saw him do many other miracles besides the ones told about in this book. But these [miracles] are recorded so that you will believe that Jesus is the Messiah, the Son of God. And when you believe this truth, you will have life. (John 20:30-31)*

RELATED VERSES: *Matthew 11:4-5; John 7:21*

RELATED QUESTIONS: *How did Jesus get the coin into the fish's mouth? How could Jesus turn water into wine? Why did Jesus try to have Peter walk on the sea? How did Jesus make demons leave people? How could Jesus feed so many people with one boy's lunch?*

Q: ARE BEATITUDES SHORT FOR BAD ATTITUDES?

not so blessed are those with bad attitudes
not so blessed are those with bad attitudes
not so blessed are those with bad attitudes
not so blessed are those with bad attitudes
not so blessed are those with bad attit...
not so blessed are those with bad att...

66

A: Jesus taught a short sermon called the Beatitudes to describe good attitudes, the attitudes that God wants us to have. The word *beatitude* means "blessed." Jesus said that whoever followed him should be poor in spirit, merciful, honest, and should expect rejection from others for being his follower. Jesus' disciples may have been thinking that they would become rich, famous, and powerful by following him, but Jesus was telling them that they should expect their rewards in heaven.

KEY VERSES: *One day, Jesus looked out and saw the crowds around him. So he went up the hillside with his disciples. He sat down and taught them there. (Matthew 5:1-2)*

RELATED VERSES: *Matthew 5:1-12*

RELATED QUESTION: *What was the most important thing that Jesus taught about?*

Q: IF JESUS DOESN'T WANT US TO GET HURT, WHY DID HE TELL US TO CHOP OUR HANDS OFF AND POKE OUR EYES OUT?

67

A: When Jesus spoke about cutting off a hand or poking out an eye, he was purposely exaggerating to make his point. This is called *hyperbole*. It's like saying, "I'd give *anything* to have an ice cream cone right now." Even though you wouldn't actually do *anything*, you want everyone to know how badly you want it. Jesus wanted to make people realize how bad sin is; it's so bad that you should get rid of *anything* that makes you sin. Jesus didn't want us actually to cut off our hands or poke out our eyes. Cutting off your hand won't get you to heaven and won't get rid of sin in your life. But saying it that way shows us how important it is to sacrifice habits, friendships, or attitudes that cause us to sin.

KEY VERSE: *"So if your hand or foot causes you to sin, cut it off and throw it away. It is better to enter Heaven crippled than to be in hell with both of your hands and feet."* (Matthew 18:8)

RELATED VERSES: *Matthew 5:29-30; 18:7-9*

NOTE TO PARENTS: *Jesus was also addressing the issue of legalism; the religious leaders were very concerned about keeping every letter of the law, and they had added hundreds of rules and regulations of their own. In effect, Jesus was saying that if they were serious about keeping the law, they should take drastic action. The point? Putting out an eye doesn't stop a child from envying his friend's bike; envy comes from the heart and involves the mind and imagination, not just what a person sees.*

Q: WHAT'S A PARABLE?

68

A: A parable is a short story with a surprise ending that makes a point. Jesus told many parables for two reasons: (1) to hide the truth from people who weren't really interested, and (2) to teach the truth to listeners who were interested and wanted to learn. Whenever Jesus told parables, those who weren't interested or who didn't want to listen didn't understand. But those who wanted to learn asked Jesus to explain the story, and then they got the point. We can learn from the Bible if we want to do what God says. But if we don't want to listen to God, the Bible won't make much sense.

KEY VERSE: *[Jesus] used many such stories to teach the people. He taught them as much as they were ready to understand. (Mark 4:33)*

RELATED VERSES: *Ezekiel 17:2; Matthew 13:34; Mark 4:9, 30-34*

NOTE TO PARENTS: *Many younger children (preadolescents) may not fully understand parables. That's OK. Part of what makes parables powerful is that they can teach us more and more as we gain experience in life. Whenever you read a parable with your children, help them see how it teaches us to live. For example, the parable of the Good Samaritan is about a hurt man who receives help from an unlikely stranger after being bypassed by two religious leaders. Simply explain that Jesus wants us to be like the helper—compassionate toward others.*

WHY DID THE DISCIPLES TELL THE PEOPLE JESUS WAS TOO BUSY TO SEE THE KIDS?

69

A: Many parents brought their children to see Jesus, and Jesus always welcomed them. The disciples tried to stop them because they didn't understand how much Jesus loved children and wanted all people to come to him. Sometimes adults act like kids aren't important or that children get in the way. But Jesus thinks kids are very important. He thinks *you* are important. Don't be afraid to bring your requests to him.

KEY VERSE: *But Jesus said, "Let the little children come to me. Don't stop them. For the Kingdom of Heaven belongs to such as these." (Matthew 19:14)*

RELATED VERSES: *Matthew 18:1-6; 19:13-15*

RELATED QUESTION: *Did Jesus talk to the kids?*

NOTE TO PARENTS: *Remember that Jesus told us to be like children in our belief in him. Watch your kids for clues about how this is done.*

Q: WHAT DOES PASSOVER MEAN?

70

A: Just before Jesus died, he had a Passover meal with his disciples. Passover is the special celebration Jews hold every year to remember when the Israelites left Egypt and started their trip to the Promised Land. Moses had told Pharaoh that because he wouldn't let the Jews go, all the firstborn boys would die. But God told the Jews to put the blood of a lamb over the door and on the sides of the door so the angel of death would see the blood and pass over them and spare the Jewish children. Today, Jews still celebrate Passover. Christians celebrate the Lord's Supper (Holy Communion) rather than Passover.

KEY VERSE: *"This yearly 'Feast of Unleavened Bread' will help you always remember today. It will remind you of the day when I brought you out of the land of Egypt. It is a law that you must celebrate this day every year, generation after generation." (Exodus 12:17)*

RELATED VERSES: *Exodus 12:1-30; Matthew 26:17-19, 26-29; 1 Corinthians 11:23-26*

RELATED QUESTIONS: *Why did they want to have the Last Supper in the house of someone they didn't know? Why did the disciples recline at the table to eat?*

NOTE TO PARENTS: *The Christian celebration of Communion comes from Jesus' celebration of Passover. Just before Jesus died, he had a Passover meal with his disciples. As they ate bread and wine, he told them that the bread was his body that would be broken for them and the wine was his blood that would be shed for them. Jesus is our Lamb that was killed; because of his blood, we can have eternal life.*

NEW TESTAMENT EVENTS AND PEOPLE

: WHY DID JUDAS BETRAY JESUS?

71

A: Judas turned against Jesus and betrayed him because Judas did not care about what Jesus had come to earth to do. Judas had hoped that Jesus would be a military leader and free the Jews from the Romans. Also, Judas loved money, and the religious leaders who wanted to kill Jesus offered Judas money to help them capture Jesus. If Judas had been one of Jesus' true disciples, he would not have betrayed him. Afterward, when he saw that Jesus was going to be killed, Judas was so upset at what he had done that he killed himself.

KEY VERSES: *Then Judas Iscariot went to the chief priests. Judas was one of the 12 apostles. He asked, "How much will you pay me to get Jesus into your hands?" They gave him 30 silver coins to do the job. From that time on, Judas watched for a chance to turn Jesus over to them. (Matthew 26:14-16)*

RELATED VERSES: *Matthew 26:47-50; John 6:70-71; 12:4-6; 13:26-30; 18:2-5*

RELATED QUESTION: *Why did Judas kill himself?*

Q: WHY WERE THE ROMAN SOLDIERS SO MEAN?

72

A: The Roman soldiers were mean for the same reason that people are mean today—they didn't love God or care about his ways. Roman soldiers were trained to keep people in line and kill if they had to. The Roman soldiers were mean to Jesus because they treated all criminals that way and they thought Jesus was a criminal just like all the others. (Some religious leaders wanted Jesus crucified because they didn't like what he was saying and because he claimed to be the Son of God.) And the soldiers felt pressure from each other; one started and the others joined in. Though the Roman authorities found Jesus innocent, they went along with the crowd and killed him on the cross, just as the prophets had predicted (see Psalm 22:18; 34:20; Zechariah 12:10).

KEY VERSE: *[The Roman soldiers] beat him on the head with a cane and spat on him. They made fun of him by bowing down to "worship" him. (Mark 15:19)*

RELATED VERSES: *Matthew 27:1-37; Mark 15:1-32; Luke 23:34-37; John 19:1-37*

RELATED QUESTIONS: *Why did Pilate let Jesus be crucified when he knew that he didn't do anything wrong? Why did the bad men make a crown for Jesus? What does* **mocked** *mean? Why did they put a staff in Jesus' hand? Why did they cast lots to get Jesus' clothes? Why did they change Jesus' robe to a purple one?*

WHY DID THE PEOPLE SAY, "COME DOWN OFF THE CROSS IF YOU ARE THE SON OF GOD"?

Gallery
Exhibit

73

A: The people who said this didn't believe in Jesus and thought he was lying when he claimed to be God. Actually, Jesus had the power to come down off the cross, but he didn't come down because he loved us and wanted to pay for our sins. When Adam and Eve sinned, everybody was separated from God. Jesus died so everyone could have the chance to be forgiven and be with God again. If Jesus had saved himself and had come off the cross, we couldn't be saved from our sins. Jesus showed his power in a much greater way—by rising from the dead three days later. Aren't you glad Jesus stayed on the cross?

KEY VERSES: *The people laughed at him as they walked by. They shook their heads in mockery. "Ha! Look at you now!" they yelled at him. "Sure, you can destroy the Temple and rebuild it in three days! If you're so wonderful, save yourself! Come down from the cross!" (Mark 15:29-30)*

RELATED VERSES: *Matthew 27:40; Luke 23:35-37*

RELATED QUESTIONS: *Why did they force Simon to carry the cross? Did they do the same thing to the two robbers that they did to Jesus? Why did people think that Jesus was calling Elijah from the cross?*

NOTE TO PARENTS: *A child's questions about Jesus' death on the cross may be a good opportunity to explain that he died for **them**, in **their** place, to pay for **their** sins. Explain that your children, individually, can trust in Jesus for salvation. You can lead them in a prayer confessing their sin, expressing trust in Jesus to save them, and thanking him for eternal life.*

NEW TESTAMENT EVENTS AND PEOPLE

Q: DID JESUS KNOW THAT HE WOULD COME TO LIFE AGAIN?

74

A: He sure did! He not only knew he would come to life again, he also told his disciples about it at least three times. But the disciples didn't seem to hear Jesus or understand what he was talking about because they were totally shocked by his death. They didn't expect Jesus to come back to life, so when they saw him, they didn't recognize him at first. But when Jesus came up close, talked with them, and ate with them, they knew it was him. After the Resurrection, Jesus appeared first to Mary Magdalene in the garden. Later, he appeared to two men walking on a road and then to the disciples gathered together in a room. He appeared to hundreds of others, too.

KEY VERSE: *"They will laugh at me and spit on me. They will beat me with their whips and kill me. But after three days I will come back to life again." (Mark 10:34)*

RELATED VERSES: *Matthew 16:21-23; 17:22-23; Mark 8:31-33; 9:30-32; 10:32-34; Luke 24:1-49; Acts 2:24; 1 Corinthians 15:3-8*

RELATED QUESTIONS: *How did the disciples recognize Jesus after he had risen from the dead? Who saw Jesus first after he came back to life?*

Q: WHY DID JESUS GO UP TO HEAVEN INSTEAD OF STAYING HERE ON EARTH?

75

A: Jesus is the Son of God, and his home is in heaven. He left his Father (and his home) to become a human being and live on the earth. So it's quite natural that Jesus would leave the earth and go back home. Jesus also went to heaven to prepare a place for us. And although Jesus left us, he also sent the Holy Spirit to take his place and be with us. Though Jesus couldn't be in two places at once, the Holy Spirit can; he can be everywhere because he lives inside all people who have trusted in Christ as Savior. Because Jesus went back to heaven, the Holy Spirit can be with you and in you, everywhere you go.

KEY VERSES: *"There are many homes in my Father's house. I am going to prepare a place for you. I will come again and take you to me. Then you will be with me where I am about to go. If this weren't so, I would tell you plainly." (John 14:2-3)*

RELATED VERSES: *Mark 16:19; Luke 24:50-51; John 14:1-7, 15-21, 25-26; 16:5-16; Acts 1:7-11*

RELATED QUESTIONS: *If Jesus is in heaven, does he still have scars on his hands, feet, and side? Why isn't Jesus here on earth now?*

DIDN'T THE TONGUES OF FIRE ON THE APOSTLES' HEADS BURN THEM?

76

A: The tongues of fire that appeared on the heads of the disciples (after Jesus had gone back to heaven) symbolized the Holy Spirit who had come into their lives. The "tongues" weren't mouth-tongues, but tongues of fire. This "fire" wasn't real fire that burns things; it looked like fire, so that's how people described it. Everyone watching knew that something very special was happening. And when they listened, they heard their own language being spoken by people who hadn't learned the language. It was obvious that God was speaking through these people.

KEY VERSES: *Then, what looked like flames of fire settled on their heads. Everyone present was filled with the Holy Spirit. They began speaking in languages they didn't even know. For the Holy Spirit gave them the ability to do this. (Acts 2:3-4)*

RELATED VERSES: *Acts 2:1-13*

RELATED QUESTIONS: *When the Holy Spirit came on the people, why were there tongues of fire on their heads? How come the sound of a wind came when the Holy Spirit came?*

Q: HOW COULD THE ANGEL UNLOCK PETER OUT OF JAIL WITHOUT KEYS?

77

A: The angel freed Peter through God's power. Herod wanted to kill Peter to make some of the other leaders happy. He had Peter arrested and sentenced to death. The night before he was going to be killed, God sent an angel to rescue Peter. He woke Peter up, and the chains fell off Peter's wrists. Then Peter and the angel walked away from the soldiers without waking any of them up. God made the iron gate open up when they walked up to it. The angel left him when they got outside. Peter could hardly believe what had happened—and neither could his friends who were praying for him! (Acts 12:12-16)

KEY VERSES: *The night before he was to be killed, he was asleep. He was chained between two soldiers. And others were standing guard by the prison gate. But suddenly there was a light in the cell! And an Angel of the Lord stood beside Peter! The Angel slapped him on the side to wake him up. Then he said, "Quick! Get up!" And the chains fell off his wrists! (Acts 12:6-7)*

RELATED VERSES: *Psalm 68:6; Acts 5:12-29*

RELATED QUESTIONS: *Why did Peter go to jail? Why did the angel let Peter out of jail?*

Q: HOW BIG WERE THE WORMS THAT ATE KING HEROD?

78

A: King Herod had become very popular with many of the people because he had been hurting the Christians. Later, some people who were trying to get on his good side told him that he looked and sounded like a god. Already a very proud man, Herod enjoyed hearing what the people said, and he accepted their worship as though he really were a god. Because Herod did this instead of honoring God, God caused him to be filled with tiny worms, or maggots, that ate him from the inside out. In the Bible, worms are a sign of pain and punishment.

KEY VERSE: *Right then, an Angel of the Lord struck Herod with a sickness. Soon he was filled with maggots and died. This was because he let the people worship him instead of giving the glory to God. (Acts 12:23)*

RELATED VERSES: *Mark 9:48; Acts 12:1-4, 20-23*

Q: HOW COULD PETER KILL AND EAT ANIMALS THAT WERE IN A VISION?

79

A: Peter never actually ate the animals he saw in his vision; he received *permission* to eat them. You see, the animals Peter saw were the types that the Jews were not supposed to eat (called "unclean" animals). In his vision, a voice told Peter to kill and eat any of the animals he wished. Peter didn't actually eat the animals that he saw because they weren't real, but soon after seeing the vision, Peter learned its meaning. Three men who weren't Jews came to the door and asked Peter to come and talk to their leader, an officer in the Roman army. Normally Peter, a Jew, would not have anything to do with non-Jews (Gentiles) because they, like the animals, were considered unclean. But the vision made him realize that he should go with the men. Because Peter obeyed God and went with the men, the Roman soldier (Cornelius), his family, and his servants all became followers of Christ.

KEY VERSES: *In the sheet were all sorts of animals, snakes, and birds. Jews were not allowed to eat any of the things that were there. Then a voice said to him, "Go kill and eat any of them you wish." (Acts 10:12-13)*

RELATED VERSES: *Acts 10:9-48*

RELATED QUESTIONS: *Why did God make Peter have that dream? What is a trance? Why did God bring a sheet of animals down?*

Q: WHY WAS IT AGAINST THE LAW TO MAKE FRIENDS WITH A GENTILE?

80

A: A Gentile was anyone who was not a Jew. It *wasn't* against the law to make friends with a Gentile. Instead, God wanted the Jewish people not to copy and be like Gentiles because they didn't follow the Jewish laws and didn't worship the true God. Some Jews wouldn't even walk through Gentile towns. Jews did accept some Gentiles into their religion. They were called "God-fearers." By breaking down this barrier, the message about Jesus could be taken to everybody, not just Jews. God wants us to accept all people and not think we're superior just because we know God.

KEY VERSE: *Peter told them, "You all know about the Jewish laws. They say it is wrong for me to come into a Gentile home like this. But God has shown me in a vision that I should never think of anyone as impure." (Acts 10:28)*

RELATED VERSES: *John 4:9; Acts 10:1–11:30; Galatians 2:11-16*

RELATED QUESTION: *What is a Gentile?*

Q: WHY WAS SAUL BLINDED BY A BRIGHT LIGHT?

81

A: At first, Saul (also known as Paul) was totally against Jesus and anyone who followed him. In fact, he watched and approved when a Christian named Stephen was killed for believing in Christ. Saul hated Christians so much that he got permission to capture them and put them in jail. But God had other plans for Saul's life. One day, while Saul was traveling to another city to look for Christians, he was blinded by a bright light. God used the light to get Saul's attention. Then Jesus appeared to him. Through this experience, Saul believed in Jesus. He became a strong follower of Christ and a great missionary. Instead of trying to get rid of Christians, he went all over the world helping people become Christians. He wrote many letters to those Christians; some of those letters are in our Bibles today.

KEY VERSES: *Saul was almost to Damascus to arrest the believers there. But suddenly a bright light from Heaven shone down on him! He fell to the ground. And he heard a voice saying to him, "Saul! Saul! Why are you trying to hurt me?" (Acts 9:3-4)*

RELATED VERSES: *Acts 7:59-60; 9:1-8; 26:1-18; Galatians 1:13-14*

RELATED QUESTION: *Which books of the Bible did Paul write?*

NOTE TO PARENTS: *Paul wrote Romans, 1 and 2 Corinthians, Galatians, Ephesians, Philippians, Colossians, 1 and 2 Thessalonians, 1 and 2 Timothy, Titus, and Philemon.*

Q: WHY DID PAUL WANT TO TELL THE ROMANS ABOUT JESUS?

82

A: Many people in Rome had become followers of Christ after visiting Jerusalem and hearing the message from the apostles there. Some had become Christians in other cities and had then moved to Rome. Paul wanted to meet these believers and encourage them in their faith. Rome was the most important city in the world at that time—the capital city of the Roman Empire. Paul knew that Christ's message had to go all over the world, and Rome would be a key place for helping to make that happen. Also, Paul was a Roman citizen, and he spoke Greek just as many people in Rome did, so he knew people would listen to him. Paul went on several trips all over the Roman Empire, including one to Rome, to tell people about Jesus.

KEY VERSE: *That night the Lord stood beside Paul. "Don't worry, Paul," he said. "You have told the people about me here in Jerusalem. In the same way, you must also be my witness in Rome." (Acts 23:11)*

RELATED VERSES: *Acts 4:27-30; 19:21; Romans 1:1–16:27*

RELATED QUESTION: *Does the book of Romans tell about the Romans who killed Jesus?*

Q: HOW DID PAUL SEND LETTERS TO CHURCHES IF THEY DIDN'T HAVE MAILBOXES?

83

A: In Paul's time, they didn't have a postal service like the one we have today. Instead, people sent letters by messengers or friends. Many of Paul's friends delivered his letters to churches. These friends included Timothy, Tychicus, and others. Paul wrote some letters, such as Philemon and Titus, to individuals. He wrote others, such as Romans and Philippians, to specific churches. And he wrote still others, such as Galatians and Colossians, to specific churches with the idea that the letters would be passed along to other churches. Paul's letters teach us about other parts of the Bible, about Jesus, about how Christians should live, and about how churches should be organized. Paul's letters have a lot to teach us!

KEY VERSE: *And remember why [the Lord] is waiting [to return]. He is giving us time to get his message of salvation out to others. Our wise and beloved brother Paul has talked about these things in his letters. (2 Peter 3:15)*

RELATED VERSES: *Galatians 6:11; Ephesians 6:21-22; Colossians 4:7-8; 2 Timothy 4:12-13; Titus 3:12; Philemon 1:12*

RELATED QUESTIONS: *If letters are only for the people they're written to, why do we read Paul's letters to other people? What did Paul say in his letters?*

 **WHY HASN'T GOD TOLD US WHEN JESUS IS COMING BACK?**

84

A:

Jesus promised his disciples (and us) that he would return to earth some day. But when they asked *when*, he told them, "Such things are not for you to know" (Acts 1:7). Rather than be concerned with when Jesus will return, we should always live as though Jesus can return at any moment. In other words, we should always do what is right and tell others about God's salvation. Although God doesn't say exactly when Christ will return, he did say that certain things need to take place first. One of these is that Christ will not come back until the Gospel has been preached to the whole world. God has promised that Jesus will return soon and every day passed is a day closer to his return.

KEY VERSE: *"But no one knows the date and hour when the end will be. Not even the angels know this. No, not even God's Son knows this. Only the Father knows." (Matthew 24:36)*

RELATED VERSES: *Matthew 24:3–25:46; 1 Thessalonians 5:23; Hebrews 10:37; James 5:7*

RELATED QUESTIONS: *When is Jesus coming back? How come we can't see Jesus today?*

Q: IS THERE CHURCH IN HEAVEN?

85

A: In heaven, we won't have churches like the ones we have on earth because everyone in heaven will be a believer in Christ, and all of us will be together in God's presence. So we will be able to talk, laugh, pray, and have fun together all the time. We won't need church buildings either. We will see Jesus in person, so we will be able to worship him all the time, not just an hour a week. There will also be angels in heaven worshiping with us. We don't know exactly what worship will be like, but it won't include announcements, the offering, Bible reading, and a sermon. It will be pure joy. Think about it—we will be able to talk directly to Moses, David, Paul, and all the other faithful and famous servants of God!

KEY VERSE: *But we are looking forward to God's promise of new heavens and a new earth. Only goodness will be there. (2 Peter 3:13)*

RELATED VERSES: *1 John 3:2; Revelation 21:1-27*

RELATED QUESTIONS: *How big is the church in heaven, if there is one? Who gets to go to heaven? When we all go to heaven, will Jesus make something else on the earth?*

NOTE TO PARENTS: *Be careful of telling kids that in heaven we get to worship God all the time. They may think that they'll be singing hymn after hymn and listening to sermon after sermon for all eternity. Be sure to explain that heaven will be fun and exciting—better than Disney World, Nintendo, or any party they can imagine.*

Q: WILL I HAVE A BEDROOM UP IN HEAVEN?

86

A: Jesus told his disciples that where his Father lived there were many homes. But we don't know exactly what that place or "house" will be like. In heaven, we will have what the Bible calls glorified bodies. In other words, our bodies will be different from what they are now. We will be able to recognize others, but we won't need food or sleep. We won't have bedrooms in heaven like the ones we have here; instead, we'll have very special places, each one prepared for us by Jesus. And we won't have to worry about the weather—the temperature will always be perfect. We won't even have to be concerned about what to wear—God will give us clothes. Heaven is a wonderful place, filled with joy, love, and happiness!

KEY VERSE: *"There are many homes in my Father's house. I am going to prepare a place for you." (John 14:2)*

RELATED VERSES: *John 14:2-4; Revelation 21:1-27*

RELATED QUESTIONS: *Will we live with our families in heaven? What do people walk on up in heaven, clouds? Will we see the twelve disciples in heaven? What kind of clothes do they have in heaven? Is it cold up in heaven? What is it like in heaven? Do people have birthdays in heaven and get older? Do people have babies up in heaven? Are there only old people in heaven?*

NOTE TO PARENTS: *Children always have questions about heaven. The questions listed above are good and indicate that they are thinking in terms of* **things** *and* **personal security.** *Let them know that heaven is a place of massive joy—they will like being there more than anywhere else. We don't know what will happen in heaven—only that it will be wonderful!*

NEW TESTAMENT EVENTS AND PEOPLE

BIBLE TIMES

WHEN DID ALL THIS HAPPEN?

87

A: Everything in the Bible happened a long time ago—hundreds and hundreds of years before your grandparents were born. In fact, when you say what year it is right now, that tells about how many years have passed since Jesus lived on earth, and that's about when the New Testament was written. But many, many years also separate the Old Testament from the New. The events described in the Old Testament took place over thousands of years, and there are four hundred years between the last event in the Old Testament and the first event in the New. Although people who lived long ago didn't have TV, cars, computers, and other modern inventions, they weren't stupid. In fact, they were a lot like us. Those things just hadn't been invented yet.

KEY VERSE: *We were helpless sinners who had no use for God. Then Christ came at just the right time and died for us. (Romans 5:6)*

RELATED VERSES: *Genesis 1:1; Exodus 1:11; 12:40; Isaiah 54:9; Hebrews 1:1-2; 4:2*

RELATED QUESTIONS: *How long ago was the Bible written? Were people who lived in Bible times stupid?*

Q: HOW DID THE PEOPLE TRAVEL?

88

A: People in Bible times didn't have cars, trains, buses, or airplanes, but they still had to travel from town to town. Usually they walked. If you've ever taken a hike, you know that you walk until you're tired, and then you rest. You may even have to pitch a tent and camp out for the night before getting to your destination. Then you start hiking again the next day. That's what people did back then whenever they walked a long way. If they could afford it, people also rode on donkeys, camels, or horses. Sometimes people (usually kings, soldiers, or rich people) would ride in chariots that were pulled by horses. And, of course, when they had to travel over water, they went in boats or ships.

KEY VERSE: *"Eat it with your traveling clothes on, prepared for a long trip. Wear your walking shoes and carry your walking sticks in your hands. Eat it quickly. This observance shall be called the Lord's Passover." (Exodus 12:11)*

RELATED VERSES: *Exodus 12:34, 37-38; 13:20; 1 Samuel 25:18; Matthew 21:1-11; Acts 1:12*

RELATED QUESTION: *Did they have trains in the olden days when Jesus was down here?*

Q: DID CHILDREN IN BIBLE TIMES COLOR?

89

A: Children in Bible times didn't color with crayons like the ones we have today, but they did draw pictures. They also played games. Archaeologists (people who study ancient cities and cultures) have found some of the games. Children back then dressed differently from the way we do, their houses and schools were made differently, and they had different kinds of games. But they were just like kids today in many ways. They liked to have fun. They had family chores to do. When they were bad, their parents disciplined them. They studied. They had times of happiness and sadness. They were real kids.

KEY VERSE: *And the streets will be filled with boys and girls at play. (Zechariah 8:5)*

RELATED VERSES: *Matthew 11:16; Ephesians 6:1-4*

RELATED QUESTIONS: *What was life like for a child back then? Were there schools for Bible children to go to? Did Jesus go to school? Did they have sinners at school when Jesus was a boy? Did people in Bible times play games?*

Q: DO PEOPLE LIVE IN THE LAND OF ISRAEL TODAY?

90

A: Today, millions of people live in the lands where the Bible events took place, including Israel. Egypt, Iraq, Jordan, and Israel are some of the nations that now make up where Abraham, Isaac, Jacob, Joseph, Moses, Joshua, Gideon, Samuel, David, Solomon, Isaiah, Jonah, and Jesus lived. The cities that Paul visited are in parts of what we know today as Turkey, Greece, and Italy. Thousands of people go to these lands every year to visit places mentioned in the Bible. Some of the people there still dress much as they did in Bible times, but the big cities are very modern, with skyscrapers, telephones, fax machines, and computers.

KEY VERSE: *"I will never leave the people of Israel or David, my servant. I will never change the plan that his child will rule the descendants of Israel. Instead I will cause them to prosper once again. And I will have mercy on them." (Jeremiah 33:26)*

RELATED VERSES: *Jeremiah 33:24-26; Matthew 28:19-20*

RELATED QUESTIONS: *Can we go and see Babylon today? Do the people in Israel today worship God? Can we visit Bible people's homes? How come the Holy Land is filled with war and unhappiness?*

NOTE TO PARENTS: *If you can find a Bible map or atlas, show your kids where this all happened. Compare it to where you live. Tell them that Israel, Jordan, and other areas are called the "Holy Land" because that's where Bible events took place, but God isn't there more than anywhere else. Jesus told the disciples to take his message to the whole world, and we can serve God anywhere.*

Q: WHY DID PEOPLE IN BIBLE TIMES BOW DOWN TO WELCOME EACH OTHER?

91

A: In Bible times, people usually greeted each other with a hug or a kiss on the cheek. That's like a handshake today. They almost never bowed down unless they wanted to show humility, service, or great respect toward someone. People always bowed before a king or another important official. But when they were just meeting on the street or visiting one another's homes, they usually just hugged or kissed.

KEY VERSE: *Shake hands for me with all the brothers there. (1 Thessalonians 5:26)*

RELATED VERSES: *Exodus 11:8; 1 Samuel 25:23; Isaiah 60:14; Luke 24:5*

Q: WHY DID PEOPLE GO TO WELLS INSTEAD OF USING THE WATER AT HOME?

92

A: In Bible times, people went to rivers, streams, wells, and cisterns for their water because they didn't have indoor plumbing. (They also used candles and lanterns at night because they didn't have electricity.) A well was a hole dug deep into the ground to an underground spring. A cistern was a huge hole in the ground that collected rain water. Many people today use wells. Water from wells and cisterns is very clean. Although the people didn't have pipes and faucets, or chlorine and fluoride in their water like we have, they had plenty of good, clean water. And God gave them rules to follow that protected their health.

KEY VERSE: *"But you don't have a bucket," she said. "And this is a very deep well! Where would you get this living water?" (John 4:11)*

RELATED VERSES: *Genesis 24:45; 26:32; 37:24; Exodus 7:24; 1 Samuel 7:6; 2 Samuel 23:15-16*

RELATED QUESTIONS: *How did they light up their houses? Did the Bible people have electricity? Did Bible people have matches? How did people in the Bible make their candles? Did they have bathtubs like ours in Bible days?*

NOTE TO PARENTS: *Don't give the impression that this was crushing poverty. Due to the Old Testament laws, things were clean and sanitary.*

Q: DID PEOPLE HAVE SHOES IN BIBLE DAYS?

93

A: Because it is very sunny, hot, and dry in the Middle East (Bible lands), people usually wore sandals rather than shoes. Their sandals, made of leather, would be fastened to the feet with strips of leather attached to the bottom and wrapped up around the shins. Sandals protected their feet without making them hot. This also meant that their feet got dirty quite easily. Whenever people entered a home, they had to clean off the dust and dirt that had stuck to their sweaty feet. That's why Jesus spoke of washing others' feet as an act of service—it was a dirty job!

KEY VERSE: *Then [Jesus] poured water into a basin and began to wash the disciples' feet. He wiped them with the towel he had around him. (John 13:5)*

RELATED VERSES: *Deuteronomy 25:9-10; Ruth 4:7-8; Ezekiel 16:9-10; Matthew 10:14; Mark 6:11; Luke 7:44; 9:5; 10:11; John 13:5-15*

RELATED QUESTIONS: *How did people get their ears pierced in Bible days? Why didn't any people in the Bible wear glasses? Did anyone wear sunglasses in the Bible?*

HOW COME THERE ARE NO BIBLE STORIES THAT TAKE PLACE IN WINTER?

94

A: Because the Bible doesn't mention snow very often, we might assume that none of the Bible stories took place in the winter. But, in fact, they took place at all times throughout the year. Bible lands are a bit too warm in the winter for snow, so that's why it's rarely mentioned. But it does rain in the winter. Though the winters aren't as cold as they are in the northern United States and Canada, there is snow on some of the mountains of Israel, especially in the northern area (where Lebanon is today).

KEY VERSE: *The snow never melts high up in the Lebanon mountains. The cold, flowing streams from the crags of Mount Hermon never run dry. (Jeremiah 18:14)*

RELATED VERSES: *Job 38:22; Psalm 51:7; Isaiah 55:10; 2 Timothy 4:21*

RELATED QUESTION: *Was there a lot of snow in Bible days in winter?*

Q: DID PEOPLE HAVE ICE CREAM IN BIBLE TIMES?

95

A: No. Ice cream was invented only about 200 years ago. But the Israelites had lots of good food to eat. Before God brought the Israelites out of slavery in Egypt, he promised Moses that he would give them "a land 'flowing with milk and honey'" (Exodus 3:8), and that's exactly what they got. Their land was very fertile, with rich soil for growing crops and grazing animals. The Hebrews had all kinds of delicious foods— figs, dates, honey, grapes, raisins, venison, bread, rice, lamb, milk, cheese, all kinds of vegetables, and other foods. They made cakes out of barley, raisins, and figs. Often they would flavor their food with salt and spices too, just as we do today. The Hebrews didn't have super-markets, microwaves, or refrigerators, but they had plenty of healthy, delicious food.

KEY VERSE: *This was [the spies'] report: "We came to the land you sent us to see. It is indeed a wonderful country! It is a land 'flowing with milk and honey.' Here is some fruit we have brought as proof." (Numbers 13:27)*

RELATED VERSES: *Genesis 1:29; 2:16-17; 9:2-4; 27:3-4; Exodus 3:8; Numbers 13:23; 1 Samuel 25:18; 2 Samuel 17:29; 1 Kings 14:3; 1 Chronicles 12:40; Proverbs 25:16; Ezekiel 4:12; Daniel 1:12-16*

RELATED QUESTIONS: *What kind of food did the Hebrews eat? Was there pepper and salt in Bible days? Did the people before the Flood have different food than we have nowadays? Did people make cookies in Bible days?*

Q: HOW COME THE HUSBANDS COULD HAVE SO MANY WIVES?

96

A: Actually, very few husbands had more than one wife. Most had only one wife and lived with their families just as people do today. But some men, usually kings or rich men, would marry several women at once. A king might marry a princess from a neighboring country, for example, to ensure peace with that country. Other men married more than one wife because their first wives couldn't have children. No matter what the reason, God never wanted men to live this way. His plan is for a man to have one wife and for a woman to have one husband. Today people don't usually have more than one wife or husband (it's against the law), but they sometimes leave or divorce their spouses. But that's also not according to God's plan.

KEY VERSE: *This explains why a man leaves his father and mother. And it tells why he is joined to his wife in such a way that the two become one person. (Genesis 2:24)*

RELATED VERSES: *Deuteronomy 25:5; Matthew 19:3-6; Ephesians 5:31*

RELATED QUESTIONS: *Were families different or the same as ours? Did the fathers bring flowers to the wives in Bible days?*

Q: WHY DID PEOPLE KILL ANIMALS FOR CHURCH?

97

A: Before Jesus came, God's people had to sacrifice animals in worship to make payment for their sins. All of us sin against God, and that sin must be paid for. The animal took the person's place. (Not all sacrifices involved killing animals; some people would offer grain as a praise offering to God.) But when Jesus came, he died for every person's sin for all time. That's why John the Baptist called him "the Lamb of God who takes away the world's sin!" (John 1:29). The sacrifice of animals in Old Testament times represented Jesus' future death for us; the animals could not actually take away sins, as Jesus could (see Hebrews 10:4-7). Because Jesus died and rose again, we never have to sacrifice animals again. Instead, we worship and praise Jesus for all he's done for us.

KEY VERSE: *But Christ gave himself for our sins as one offering for all time. Then he sat down in the place of highest honor by God's right hand. (Hebrews 10:12)*

RELATED VERSES: *Genesis 4:4; Leviticus 17:3-5, 11; John 1:29; Hebrews 9:22; 10:1-18*

RELATED QUESTIONS: *Why did people worship idols in the Bible? How come idols were always cows and sheep? Why don't we have temples and palaces nowadays?*

NOTE TO PARENTS: *Kids are going to be repulsed at the idea of killing, but they would also be appalled if they found out where they get their hamburger, the details of which we hide from them. Actually, most of the meat sacrificed to God was given to the priests and Levites for food.*

Q: DID PEOPLE IN BIBLE TIMES HAVE MUSIC?

98

A: People had music in Bible times and loved it! Although they didn't have compact discs, tapes, pianos, or electric guitars, they did have many kinds of instruments. They also loved to sing. Singing praise to God was a very important part of their worship. They also sang songs to express their feelings. (All of the Psalms are songs—150 of them.) Often dirges (sad songs) would be sung when people were very sad. Perhaps the most well-known musician in the Bible is King David. He played the harp and wrote many songs, some of which are in the book of Psalms.

KEY VERSES: *Sing your praises to him! Sing with music from the harp. Let the cornets and trumpets shout! Make a joyful noise before the Lord, the King! (Psalm 98:5-6)*

RELATED VERSES: *Exodus 15:1-21; 1 Samuel 19:9; 2 Samuel 1:17-27; Psalm 57:7; 92:1; 98:1-9; 144:9, 150:3-5*

RELATED QUESTIONS: *If David wasn't a good songwriter would God still have asked him to write the Psalms? Were there pianos in the Bible days?*

Q: WERE THERE ANY CRIMES IN THE BIBLE?

99

A: Ever since Adam and Eve sinned against God, sin, and therefore crime, has been in the world. In fact, every person ever born has been born a sinner. That means that it is natural for boys, girls, men, and women to do wrong—to lie, cheat, steal, and hurt others. So crimes have been committed by people since the beginning. That's why we need Jesus. Only Jesus can take away our sin, teach us to do right, and help us love and respect one another. It all starts when we admit our sin, ask Jesus to forgive us, and invite him to rule our lives. If everyone did that and tried to obey God, there would be a lot less crime in the world!

KEY VERSE: *Meanwhile, the crime rate was rising rapidly across the earth. As seen by God, the world was rotten to the core. (Genesis 6:11)*

RELATED VERSES: *Genesis 6:1-11; 38:1-30; Matthew 6:19; Luke 23:38-43; 1 Corinthians 6:10*

RELATED QUESTIONS: *Were there any wars in the Bible days?*

Q: WHAT LANGUAGE DID THEY SPEAK IN BIBLE DAYS?

100

A: At one time, everyone in the world spoke the same language. But they became proud and thought they were as good as God. When they tried to build a tower to heaven (the Tower of Babel), God gave them all different languages. That caused them to become confused, so they quit the project and scattered all over the earth. Ever since then, in Bible times just as today, each different group of people has spoken a different language. The most common languages the people of the Bible spoke were Hebrew, Aramaic, and Greek. In heaven, there will be people "from every nation" (Revelation 5:9).

KEY VERSES: *"How can this be?" they exclaimed. "For these men are all from Galilee. But we hear them speaking the languages of the lands where we were born!" (Acts 2:7-8)*

RELATED VERSES: *Genesis 11:1-9; 2 Kings 18:26-28; Ezra 4:7; Isaiah 19:18; 36:11-13; Daniel 2:4; John 19:17-20; Acts 2:6-11; 6:1; 9:29; 21:37-40; 22:2; 26:14; Revelation 9:11*

RELATED QUESTIONS: *What was the first language people had before God changed all of the languages? How come the people in the Bible have such weird names?*

Q: DOES GOD HAVE THINGS TO DO AT NIGHTTIME?

...PLEASE HELP US NOT HAVE TO WAKE UP
AT NIGHT, AND DON'T LET LOUD NOISES HAPPEN,
AND HELP THE CAT CATCH ALL THE MICE,
AND DON'T LET MY DAD SNORE SO LOUD
THAT HE WAKES UP MY MOM, AND HELP
OUR BRAINS TO KEEP ON WORKING EVEN
THOUGH WE HAVE THEM TURNED OFF, AND...

101

A: God does not have a body like ours, so he does not need to sleep. And because God is everywhere and lives in eternity, there's no night or day for him (and when it's night here, it's day somewhere else). So God is always working when we are sleeping. When you go to sleep, you can be sure that God is awake, watching over you and taking care of you.

KEY VERSES: *[God] will never let me stumble, slip, or fall. For he is always watching, never sleeping. (Psalm 121:3-4)*

RELATED VERSE: *1 Kings 18:27*

Q: DOES GOD HAVE A SENSE OF HUMOR?

102

A: Yes. One clue that God has a sense of humor is that men, women, boys, and girls love to laugh. Genesis 1:26-27 says that God created human beings in his image. That means that in many ways we are like God—and he is like us. So if we have a sense of humor, God probably does, too. What's more, in his Word, God talks quite a bit about joy, happiness, fun, and laughter: "Sarah said, 'God has brought me laughter!'" (Genesis 21:6); "How we laughed and sang for joy!" (Psalm 126:2); "When people are gloomy, everything seems to go wrong. When they are cheerful, everything seems right!" (Proverbs 15:15); "Always be full of joy in the Lord. I'll say it again—rejoice!" (Philippians 4:4). It is clear that God wants his people to enjoy life.

But the fact that God has a sense of humor doesn't mean that he enjoys all the things that we think are funny or that he likes all our jokes. Some people are cruel with their humor; they laugh when people are hurt, or they make fun of others. That's wrong. We should laugh *with* people, not at them. Tell good jokes, laugh, enjoy life; God wants you to be filled with joy.

KEY VERSE: *A cheerful heart does good like medicine. (Proverbs 17:22)*

RELATED VERSES: *Psalm 2:4; 37:12-13; Ecclesiastes 3:4; 1 Thessalonians 5:16; 1 Peter 1:8*

Additional books from
The Livingstone Corporation

101 QUESTIONS CHILDREN ASK ABOUT GOD 0-8423-5102-7
Concise, thoughtful, easy-to-explain answers to some of the most
important questions kids will ever ask.

CHOICE ADVENTURES SERIES Volumes 1–16
By exploring the many plot possibilities in these humorous adventure
stories, kids will learn about wise decision making, positive values,
and trust in God.